CONCISE
LINCOLN
LIBRARY

—

EDITED BY RICHARD W. ETULAIN
AND SYLVIA FRANK RODRIGUE

BRIAN R. DIRCK

Lincoln in Indiana

Southern Illinois University Press
Carbondale

Southern Illinois University Press
www.siupress.com

20   19   18   17   4   3   2   1

The Concise Lincoln Library has been made possible
in part through a generous donation by the Leland E.
and LaRita R. Boren Trust.

Volumes in this series have been published with support from the Abraham Lincoln Bicentennial Foundation, dedicated to perpetuating and expanding Lincoln's vision for America and completing America's
unfinished work.

Jacket illustration adapted from a painting by
Wendy Allen

Library of Congress Cataloging-in-Publication Data
Names: Dirck, Brian R., 1965– author.
Title: Lincoln in Indiana / Brian R. Dirck.
Description: Carbondale : Southern Illinois University
Press, 2017. | Series: Concise Lincoln library | Includes
bibliographical references and index.
Identifiers: LCCN 2016026534 | ISBN 9780809335657
(cloth : alk. paper) | ISBN 9780809335664 (e-book)
Subjects: LCSH: Lincoln, Abraham, 1809–1865—
Childhood and youth. | Lincoln, Abraham, 1809–1865
—Travel—Indiana. | Presidents—United States—
Biography.
Classification: LCC E457.32 .D57 2017 | DDC 973.7092
[B] —dc23
LC record available at https://lccn.loc.gov/2016026534

Printed on recycled paper. ♻
This paper meets the requirements of ANSI/NISO
Z39.48-1992 (Permanence of Paper) ∞

For Doug Nelson, my first Indiana friend

CONTENTS

Gallery of illustrations beginning on page 51

A NOTE ON SOURCES

The documents in the Herndon-Weik collection are a combination of oral interviews, usually transcribed by William Herndon and Jesse Weik, and written statements and letters by eyewitnesses that were collected by Herndon and Weik for their project. In quoted material from the oral interview transcriptions, I have chosen to silently correct spelling and grammatical errors, as these reflect the particular idiosyncrasies of the interviewer rather than the interviewee. I have also taken the liberty to make alterations in punctuation, capitalization, and minor style points in those sources where I found it necessary to do so for clarity's sake. In material from statements and letters written directly by eyewitnesses, I have preserved the original spelling and grammar.

LINCOLN IN INDIANA

PROLOGUE

Abraham Lincoln lived in the state of Indiana for nearly one-quarter of his life, from 1816 until 1830. When he arrived he was a child; when he left he was nearly a grown man, on the cusp of adulthood and independence. Those Indiana years were critical to his development as a person. But they are also a difficult period in Lincoln's life for historians to analyze and accurately describe.

The most authoritative voice on the subject, Lincoln himself, is largely silent. He rarely spoke of or wrote about his early years, aside from passages in three brief autobiographies he produced between 1858 and 1860, mainly for political purposes. Those three documents combined number approximately four thousand words, and the parts that directly address his life in Indiana amount to less than eight hundred words—awfully thin gruel, at best.[1]

Lincoln might have been inclined toward silence because he was frankly embarrassed by his poor upbringing and circumstances. He used his "rail-splitter" image and humble roots to good political effect when need be but otherwise harbored no romantic illusions about his origins. "It is a great piece of folly to attempt to make anything out of me or my early life," he told a Chicago newspaperman during the 1860 presidential campaign. "It can all be condensed into a single sentence, . . . 'The short and simple annals of the poor.' That's my life, and that's all you or anyone else can make out of it."[2]

Lincoln did not particularly want people to know about his Indiana roots, and his wishes would have remained fulfilled if not for his law partner, William Herndon. After Lincoln's death Herndon set out to write what he hoped would be the definitive biography of his friend. Billy had grown increasingly annoyed by the insistence of Lincoln's many admirers on excessively lionizing the martyred president. "He was not God," Herndon grumbled, and "he was not perfect. . . . It is my intention to write out this *Life* of Mr. L[incoln] honestly [and] fairly—impartially if I can."[3]

To that end, and with the help of a sympathetic lawyer and news-paperman named Jesse Weik, Herndon undertook the difficult task of tracking down and interviewing anyone he could find who knew Lincoln, dating back to his childhood days in Indiana and Kentucky: friends, relatives, neighbors, business and political associates. Those hundreds of interviews and letters formed the backbone for Billy's 1889 biography, *Herndon's Lincoln*, and they became an indispensable resource for nearly every modern Lincoln biography thereafter. In 1998 Lincoln scholars Douglas L. Wilson and Rodney O. Davis performed the great service of collecting and annotating the entire collection into a single volume, *Herndon's Informants*.

The documents in this collection constitute the bulk of primary source evidence available on Lincoln's life in Indiana, and they form the backbone of this book. In fact, were it not for the Herndon-Weik collection, we would know so very little about Lincoln's Indiana life that this book would be nearly impossible to write. But with all due respect to Herndon and Weik, their collection is problematic; it both informs and bedevils Lincoln scholars.

The people Herndon and Weik interviewed were usually elderly men and women who struggled to remember events decades old, and they suffered inevitable lapses in memory and confusion regarding details. They mixed up dates, misremembered names, and sometimes contradicted themselves and each other. Their testimony was also inevitably colored by the biases and agendas of their interviewers; Herndon in particular harbored certain deeply held opinions about Lincoln's views on religion, relationship with Mary, intellect, and character, which in turn shaped the sorts of questions he asked and sometimes distorted the answers he received.

Everyone was also aware that in knowing Abraham Lincoln, they had brushed elbows with greatness. Many of the key interviews related to Lincoln's Indiana years were conducted by Herndon in late 1865 and early 1866, just months removed from Lincoln's tragic assassination. Most of the interviewees harbored a fresh image of Lincoln's martyrdom in their minds. These were often ordinary people who had lived ordinary lives; recording their brief encounters with Lincoln, even when he was just a boy growing up on the Indiana frontier, was their only chance to at least briefly be part of something larger than themselves. They were therefore understandably prone to embellishment and exaggeration of both the young Lincoln's good qualities and their own roles in shaping his character.

With all of this in mind, I have tried to exercise due caution with the Herndon-Weik collection, maintaining a healthy respect for its limitations. Wherever possible, I have tried to carefully weigh each document's logical consistency, the interviewee's veracity, and the consistency of his or her testimony with other available sources. I have also attempted to set the testimony within the larger context of early Indiana's history and the general social and cultural milieu of early nineteenth-century America.

What emerges is an admittedly imperfect portrait of Lincoln in Indiana. So many questions remain unanswered and are in all probability unanswerable. We know very little, for example, regarding Lincoln's relationship with his sister or his mother, or what exactly Lincoln thought of his cousin Dennis Hanks, whose testimony in the Herndon-Weik collection is so crucial. I often found it necessary to tell Lincoln's story by focusing more on the people and places surrounding him, rather than Lincoln himself.

But however imperfect our understanding of Lincoln in Indiana, it is a vitally necessary aspect of any investigation into his life. Any person's character is indelibly shaped by childhood and youth; not for nothing are these often referred to as one's "formative years." How the adult Lincoln later understood kinship, friendship, work and play, religion and education, parenting and childhood—all were influenced by those days in Indiana about which he preferred not to speak or write.

In 1859 Lincoln added to one of his autobiographies a brief introduction apologizing for its brevity. "Herewith is a little sketch, as you requested," he wrote to the recipient, his friend and political ally Jesse W. Fell. "There is not much of it, for the reason, I suppose, that there is not much of me." When it came to his Indiana years, Lincoln was mistaken; far more of him came from those Hoosier woods than he perhaps realized.[4]

BEGINNINGS

Sometime during the late fall of 1816, a ferry boat docked on the Ohio River's northern shore a few miles west of the little town of Troy, Indiana, at a place called Thompson's Ferry, where the Anderson River empties into the Ohio.[1] The Anderson is narrow, only about fifty to sixty yards wide, and windswept enough that it sometimes forced landings farther downriver. But its current was sufficient to power at least one mill, and its confluence with the Ohio created a useful landing spot, well worn from migrants and their livestock making their way into Indiana's interior.[2]

"The country was very rough," remembered a local farmer, the landscape crinkled with shallow valleys and low hills; the area around Thompson's Ferry was nicknamed by locals "the pocket." The place was thickly carpeted with trees, "gum, beech, poplar, hickory, walnut, ash, and various kinds of oak." The leaves were largely gone at this point, and the early morning and evening air would have contained a frigid bite, coating the tree limbs and underbrush with a liberal dusting of ice. There was enough of a chill to lend a bit of urgency to the raft's occupants. Winter was coming.[3]

Perhaps the flatboat's occupants were also worried about suffering a good ducking in the Ohio, swollen and muddy as it was from the fall rains. They had spent several days waiting on the Kentucky bank with several other families, hoping for the swift-moving waters to settle a bit. The crossing could be dangerous, particularly if the river was at or near flood stage. Fortunately for the emigrants, the

Thompson's Ferry rig was a licensed affair, bonded by the state of Indiana and requiring at least two competent operators.[4]

Crowded onto the flatboat were a pair of feather beds—prized possessions for any wilderness family—two horses, possibly a cow or two, clothing, and household bric-a-brac, along with some carpentry and other tools. This probably left little room to move for the family of five clustered around their belongings, along with the ferry's crew.[5]

Either holding the horses steady to calm them or helping guide the vessel across the river, or some combination of both, was Thomas Lincoln, age thirty-eight. He was invariably described by friends and family as stocky or "square built," with a dark complexion, "strong and muscular." He had a frank farmer's countenance with a "re-markable large roman nose" and moved slowly and deliberately. As he crossed into Indiana that day, his eyes perhaps squinting at the approaching shoreline, Thomas likely was dressed as other farmers of the time, with a wool coat to keep out the chill, a "slouch" hat of some sort, and heavy homemade leather boots or brogans. It was not entirely unfamiliar; he had visited Indiana before, though not with his entire family and worldly goods in tow.[6]

His wife, Nancy, was several years younger. She was about five feet seven inches tall, with "a spare delicate frame," pale skin, hazel eyes, and dark hair. A friend later described her as possessing "sharp features," an angular chin with a high forehead, and a piercing, intelligent gaze—rather a contrast to her husband's stony thickness. Maybe she stood next to Thomas on the raft that morning, holding one of the horses' reins and likewise peering intently at the approaching shore.[7] Unlike Thomas, Nancy had never before set foot in Indiana.

Neither had their two children, both also standing on the crowded raft, probably wide-eyed at the whole process of moving and the prospect of a new home. Sarah, or "Sally," was ten, "quick minded," and diligent. She had very dark brown, possibly black, hair and a dark complexion, and she would later be described as "heavy built"—a mix of her father and mother.[8]

Her little brother, Abraham, was eight, a "long tall raw boned boy" who also exhibited the family traits of dark skin, hair, and eyes. More than one person used the word "gawky" to describe him, then and later, as he had the awkward sort of build that foreshadowed his growth into an inordinately tall manhood. He probably wore buckskin pants, a tow-linen shirt, and possibly a slouch hat or coonskin cap.[9]

Rounding out the party was the nineteen-year-old Dennis Hanks, Nancy's first cousin. There is no extant description of him at the time, but in later years he was physically stout, with a thin, downward-turning mouth and the Hanks family's black hair and high forehead. He seems to have been a rather talkative, gregarious sort, someone who would have been jabbering away as the raft drew nearer the shore.[10]

Altogether, there was nothing remarkable about the little party. People had long been migrating northward into Indiana after either traveling down or crossing the Ohio River. They tended to be on the impoverished side, farmers who could not afford the higher land prices in Kentucky and sought cheaper alternatives on the far banks of the Ohio, some purchasing their land outright and others "squatting" without clear title, hoping to scrape together enough cash to buy their acreage before someone came along and ran them off.[11]

By 1816 the Lincolns and others like them were at the leading edge of the latest tide of farmer emigrants that had been lapping steadily westward since the seventeenth century. The tide was large and powerful, and no one could really stop it; too many people were moving too quickly into northern America for any obstacle, geographic or otherwise, to create much of a barrier. At one time it was thought the Appalachians, the largest mountain range on the eastern half of the continent, might do the trick, but following the American Revolution, the tide of emigrants washed quickly over the Appalachians and steadily poured down the Ohio River valley.

The emigrants had a natural propensity for following rivers, usually a faster and safer means of travel than overland, and the Ohio was one of the biggest of them all. It was "the most beautiful river on earth," thought Thomas Jefferson, and of immense practical benefit as a grand sluiceway for the emigrant tide.[12] No one knows exactly how many people took advantage of the opportunity; they must have numbered in the many thousands by 1816.

But that could be a problem, at least from the perspective of the new American government. Since the first English settlers had arrived in North America, they had constantly clashed with Native Americans, European fellow travelers, and each other in their pell-mell scramble west. The tide's momentum resulted in conflicting land claims, irregular boundaries, and inconsistent government policies—or no policies at all.

The Founding Fathers wanted the federal government rather than the states in charge of regulating the great western wave. Congress accordingly passed in 1790 the Southwest Ordinance, organizing the lands south of the Ohio: chiefly the future states of Kentucky and Tennessee. Three years earlier Congress had created the Northwest Ordinance for the Ohio's northern banks. The primary difference between the two was slavery, which the Southwest Ordinance allowed but the Northwest Ordinance did not. Migrants could head west down the Ohio River and turn left for the "peculiar institution," right for free soil.

But matters were not nearly so simple. In fact, nothing about the Ohio valley region, or Indiana in particular, was simple. Thomas Lincoln was placing himself and his family in a complex, difficult, and challenging environment when crossing the Ohio River that cold morning in 1816.

Originally the federal government designated as Indiana Territory nearly the entire Northwest Ordinance's expanse of land, wrapping around the western Great Lakes to the Mississippi River's eastern bank. No one really expected such an unwieldy region—nearly 260,000 square miles—to remain a single entity, so as each section filled with people and applied for statehood, Indiana Territory was steadily whittled down, first in 1803 by the creation of the new state of Ohio, two years later Michigan, and then four years after that Illinois. Indiana Territory with its modern boundaries was only seven years old in 1816; it would officially become a state right about the time the Lincolns arrived.

Everything around them was raw and feral, "a wild region," as Abraham later recalled.[13] The federal census of 1820 listed an Indiana population of approximately 147,000 people—an incredible number, given that only a little over 5,600 people had lived in the area twenty years earlier—but population growth did not necessarily fuel development.[14] Those 147,000 people, soon to be dubbed Hoosiers, were largely farmers scattered on small homesteads around the state, connected by nothing that remotely resembled a transportation network.[15] Major waterways like the Wabash, the state's primary river, were extremely difficult to ford and serviced by few reliable ferries. The roads, such as they were, barely allowed passage through Indiana's dense wilderness. "The woods were very thick with brush and undergrowth," remembered one Hoosier, "our traveling all had to be done on foot or horseback; if we would have had buggies we could not have used them."[16]

Towns tended to be tiny and inconsequential places, hamlets and villages scattered here and there. Even the state capital at Corydon, population three hundred and just fifteen miles from the Ohio River, was little more than a collection of log cabins punctuated by an occasional brick or stone building; the capitol building itself was a simple structure with forty-foot-square limestone walls. It all possessed a decidedly sleepy air; one observer called Corydon "an easy-going, old-fashioned Virginia village."[17]

Indiana's population trended young, and with good reason; it could be a dangerous place, where older people hesitated to venture. The state teemed "with many bears and other wild animals still in the woods," according to Abraham Lincoln. Panthers posed a particularly serious threat. A resident of Sprinkles Settlement in southern Indiana's Warrick County, not far from where the Lincolns would settle, recalled an incident in which a young girl was set upon by several panthers when she unwisely wandered off into the nearby woods alone. A search party from the settlement followed the sounds of unearthly screams and came upon her remains in a clearing, where a female panther, "after she had killed the girl, was teaching the young ones how to attack their prey, and she would bound onto the prostrate form [of the girl] and bite and scratch it. The kittens would go through the same motions and thus had torn her into pieces."[18]

Leaving a settled area and braving the Indiana wilderness was a chancy undertaking, irrespective of wild animals. Simply getting from one place to another presented daunting challenges. "There are but few bridges," noted a man who was trying to get to Terre Haute on the state's western marches. "One thing makes it more difficult in these lower countrys [sic], when the river once rises, they retain their height a long time."[19] Traveling on Indiana's rivers could also pose problems. We "are assending [*sic*] the Wabash," wrote a woman named Lydia Bacon, who with her husband and other companions was making her way into Indiana in the fall of 1811; "it is very difficult to assend these rivers, the current is against us and is very strong. . . . what makes it more difficult the river Wabash, is full of snags, sawyers and Sandbars." Possibly drowning in the Wabash aside, Mrs. Bacon worried about other hazards lurking in the Indiana countryside: "The night air is very damp and if exposed to it we are in danger of fever Ague."

There was also the possibility of an accident occurring in the Indiana woods that could leave one in a bad way and far from medical help. Bacon wrote of a man in her party who had "been burnt with powder. . . . he was priming his gun for the purpose of shooting some wild fowl [when] the pan took fire from the flint coming in contact and the [gunpowder] Flask which held a half pound and was nearly full, exploded, and the contents went immediately into his face, he shrieked and putting his hands to his face took the skin entirely off." There was not much the unfortunate man's friends could do, stuck as they were far from any settlement, other than apply a homemade poultice and hope for the best. He survived and kept his eyesight—a serious concern for a while—but no doubt bore the scars the rest of his life.[20]

The people who braved such dangers were a curious brew of many different cultural elements. Indiana possessed a slight French tone, France once having claimed the land as part of its larger hold on what it called New France, a huge swath of the New World stretching all the way to Canada. The British wrested this away during the French and Indian War in the mid-eighteenth century, but not before French fur trappers and traders had established several villages and forts, many of which still possessed French names when the Lincolns arrived: Vincennes, Terre Haute, French Town (later Fort Wayne), and French Lick, a fur traders' outpost located near a large salt lick.

The French themselves often adopted—or mangled—Native American names for various Indiana locations and geographic features. The Wabash River bore the Miami Indian name for "the Stream," *Wa-ba-shi-ki*, which the French sometimes wrote as Ouabache.[21] The Miami was the chief tribe here, but the area also had elements of the

Illini and Shawnee, as well as a smattering of Iroquois, Kickapoo, Lenape, Wyandotte, and Potawatomi. Even the broader cultural Native American groups could constitute a variety of smaller subgroups, local varieties of tribes that varied in their belief systems and practices. The Shawnee, for example, included people who came from Delaware tribes with whom they had intermingled when they settled in southern Indiana.[22]

The Shawnee were relative newcomers to the area, having been shoved into the Indiana region by conflicts with other Native Americans and American farmers in Ohio. For many Native Americans, Indiana was more a place to visit than to settle. Iroquois war parties frequently crisscrossed the area in the seventeenth and early eighteenth centuries, discouraging other tribes from establishing a more permanent presence. Southern Indiana was settled by Native Americans who often wintered across the Ohio River in Kentucky, or sometimes vice versa, crossing back and forth to hunt and fish. Added to this was the general cumulative effect of disease, war, and the constant pressures exerted by the new U.S. government on tribes to cede their lands by treaty and move westward, all of which combined to give Indiana's Native American populace a highly diverse, unstable quality.[23]

This was also true of the settlers arriving in Indiana from the United States. Described invariably as Indiana's white population, new arrivals like the Lincolns were not nearly as homogenous as that label implied. Many were English in origin, but the settlers also included quite a few Scotch and Irish, and even a light peppering of Welsh, Polish, and Scandinavians. The state attracted large numbers of Germans, among them a contingent of German Lutherans who created in 1814 a settlement called Harmony (later New Harmony), which later became the hub of a utopian community designed by socialist reformer Robert Owen. There were pockets of French and French Canadians (remnants of Indiana's days as part of New France) and a small collection of Swiss settlers in the area around the town of Vevay in southeastern Indiana. The Swiss brought their winemaking skills to the region and established a reputation for excellent wine "made from the Maderia and Clarret [*sic*] grapes." The surrounding area was in fact later dubbed Switzerland County.[24]

Southern culture was common in Indiana, especially in the region along and just north of the Ohio River. This was understandable, given that so many of the people living in the area hailed from Kentucky and other points to the south. Most were not aristocrats of the moonlight-and-magnolias variety; they came, rather, from the upper South, with relatively few slaves and even fewer large slave plantations. They brought with them southern customs and folkways, ranging from dialect (some theories have the word *Hoosiers* originating from a southern pronunciation of "Who's there?") to clothing, food, and drink.[25]

This southern flavoring made even the ostensibly clear line between free and slave labor problematic. Indiana had its share of antislavery people, many of whom migrated into the state from New England and various points overland, north of the Ohio River. But plenty of other Hoosiers came from southern areas where they had at least tolerated slavery as an everyday fact of life. Some came to Indiana because they wanted to live in a place without human bondage, but others were indifferent, and still others thought they could re-create Indiana as a slave state.

In 1803 some Indiana residents, with the support of territorial governor William Henry Harrison, called a convention that petitioned Congress to lift the Northwest Ordinance's slavery ban. The convention's proslavery members felt they were at a disadvantage trying to compete against products created with slave labor in southern markets, and some worried that proslavery emigrants were bypassing Indiana entirely to settle in other areas where the peculiar institution existed, such as Missouri. Congress refused to act on the petition, but Harrison and other state government officials often looked the other way when some early settlers from the South brought their slaves with them into the territory. According to the 1820 census, 237 slaves were living in ostensibly free Indiana, even though Indiana's first state constitution had formally outlawed the practice four years earlier. Free soil Indiana would remain, at least on paper, and the number of slaves living in the state steadily dwindled. Even so, well into the nineteenth century it was not unheard of for white Hoosiers living on isolated farms along the Ohio River to keep black laborers in bondage.[26]

With all these different people thrown together in Indiana, the constant potential for conflict existed. "Yankee" Hoosiers who dominated central and northern Indiana often did not much care for their southern-bred compatriots living closer to the Ohio River. Both northern- and southern-bred people in turn found the state's German contingent to be standoffish and even rude. Despite its name, Harmony rubbed many in the rest of the state the wrong way, with its dual-language English and German newspaper, its citizens' reluctance to talk to strangers, and its later conversion to New Harmony and Robert Owen's radical ideas about same-sex education and universal equality.[27]

Some of this distrust and abrasiveness shaded into outright violence; by 1816 Indiana had already seen its share of mayhem. The chief source was, predictably enough, difficulties between European settlers and Native Americans. Indiana's explosive population growth created endless opportunities for friction between "white" and "red" people who often did not like, respect, or fully understand each other. All too often these encounters turned bloody, especially in the months immediately preceding an organized rebellion in 1810 led by the Shawnee Tecumseh. Describing an incident involving a band of Native Americans, a Frenchman, and a settler named Liberty White, an army officer stationed at Fort Wayne laconically noted, "White received two balls through his body; nine stab wounds with a knife to his breast and one to his hip; his throat was cut from ear to ear. . . . The Frenchman was only shot through the neck, and scalped."[28]

Governor Harrison built a political career on his battlefield victory over Tecumseh at Tippecanoe in northern Indiana in 1811. A year later war with Britain torched native-white relations anew, with the British arming tribal warriors and urging them to assault settlers, many of whom fled. "Most of the citizens of this country have abandoned their farms, and have taken refuge in such temporary forts as they have been able to construct," Harrison noted in May 1812. Those unlucky enough to get caught out in the open wilderness often suffered brutal consequences. "A colonel [John] Small has just arrived from the Settlement on the Embarras River five miles west of this place," Harrison wrote to Secretary of War William Eustis from Vincennes, "with the information of the murder of another family by the Indians. . . . what other course is there left for us to pursue but to make a war of exterpation [*sic*] upon them?. . . . It is impossible Sir to give you an adequate Idea of the alarm and distress which these murders have produced."[29]

The fight with Tecumseh and the War of 1812 made Indiana a dark and bloody ground, and memories were long. When the Lincolns arrived, Tecumseh had been dead for three years, killed in battle near Detroit in 1813, and the war ended a year later. But stories of Native American atrocities—many greatly exaggerated or utterly false—continued to resonate. "I do not like the thought of being scalped by our Red bretheren [*sic*]," Lydia Bacon wrote while living in a military fort near Vincennes, for "they are deceitful in the extreme."[30]

Still, the lure of cheap land in Indiana overrode such fears. The very fact that the state was so slow in developing any sort of infrastructure kept land prices low. The quality of the land varied from excellent to fair—"my land is good, but not like that of old Kentuck," claimed a Hoosier farmer—depending on where in the state it was located. Indiana's tough countryside, where it was necessary to hack away the timber and undergrowth to create passable paths, likewise posed a formidable challenge to men and women wielding only axes and shovels. "The clearing away of surplus forest was the great task," Lincoln later recalled. Farmers also needed to create clear and level fields for planting—again, a daunting, time-consuming task.[31]

Farming in 1816 meant primarily subsistence agriculture, growing crops to meet the needs of a family for day-to-day life. A typical Indiana farm was small, around eighty acres, and hosted a mishmash of crops and animals, supplying the family with buckwheat, potatoes, squash, pumpkins, cabbage, beans, corn, and other vegetables or fruits compatible with the season, along with whatever a dairy cow or a bevy of chickens might produce, supplemented by wild game when possible. Labor was performed almost entirely by strong hands and backs, along with a draft animal or two.[32]

Many Indiana farmers complemented their agriculture with a secondary skill of some sort that could bring a bit of money or bartered goods on the side: blacksmithing perhaps, or carpentry, possibly the construction of a small mill if the farm site was suitable. Some would round up the wild hogs roaming loose everywhere in the nearby woods—no small task, since some of the animals could reach 250 pounds or more—and drive them to market for slaughter. Others planted fields of crops such as wheat, corn, and cotton not for consumption but for sale in Cincinnati or even the faraway markets in New Orleans. The barter and especially the money earned from these endeavors mattered; very little actual cash or coin changed hands in the state's economy, but that made money all the more precious.[33]

Some Americans such as Thomas Jefferson endlessly extolled the independence and virtues of the sturdy American subsistence farmer, who did not need money and who built and grew all he possessed with his own rough, honest hands, beholden to nobody and dependent on nothing. "Those who labor in the earth are the chosen people of God," he enthused. "Corruption of morals in the mass of cultivators is a phenomenon of which no age or nation has furnished an example," because "cultivators," unlike, say, factory workers or day laborers, knew dependence on no one, and "dependence begets subservience and venality, suffocates the germ of virtue, and prepares fit tools for the designs of ambition. . . . While we have land to labor then, let us never wish to see our citizens occupied at a workbench, or twirling a distaff."[34]

But Jefferson was more than a little naive—the man had never actually gotten much dirt under his fingernails working a plow or planting a field, after all—and subsistence farming in a place like Indiana was a chancy affair. Hoosiers were at the mercy of potentially violent confrontations with Native Americans, land disputes with each other, capricious weather, voracious insects and other vermin, the vagaries of soil depletion and exhaustion (which was little understood in 1816), and sometimes just plain bad luck. Living in remote areas, their almost Herculean efforts at clearing the forest having produced a bald spot among the trees where they could build a cabin and plant a crop, Indiana farmers often felt not so much heroic as terribly isolated. "So dense was the forest that the only evidence of other occupied farms nearby was the sound of an axe, the crowing fowls or barking watch-dog," recalled one.[35]

Nor was Jefferson's vision of the happily independent farmer toiling away blissfully unaffected by market capitalism entirely accurate.

At one time America's subsistence farmers may have more or less fit into this romantic vision of tough independence, but by the early nineteenth century that time was passing. Whether they entirely willed it or not, America's small farmers were being steadily enmeshed in an ever more complex and far-reaching market economy, its tendrils reaching out to the far corners of the rapidly expanding new nation. In 1816 that market economy was still very much local, especially in places like Indiana, with clusters of little trade networks and exchanges in farming communities and small villages.

From such humble beginnings would a burgeoning national marketplace eventually thrive by the 1850s, but when the Lincolns arrived the foundation was there, as well as the desire. Most Hoosiers may have been subsistence farmers, but they did not necessarily want to remain so. They wanted to earn money, the better to improve their lot in life: replace that gunny sack over the window with store-bought glass, buy the wife a manufactured dress to replace her homespun garment, maybe purchase a better-quality plow to cut through the stiff Indiana soil. Those isolated farmers who were busy carving farms out of the Indiana brush would take all the help they could get.[36]

Most important, they wanted to buy and own their land, free and clear. Even squatters were not terribly enamored of squatting: land-ownership was everything. Quite a few Indiana farmers had migrated to the state because they believed their odds of acquiring clear title to their farms were better north of the Ohio River. States in the upper South like Kentucky carried a well-deserved reputation for shoddy surveying and bookkeeping; many an upper South farmer had lost land he thought he owned free and clear because of such difficulties. The farmers hoped the new state of Indiana would be different.[37]

As a rule, settlement in Indiana moved from south to north, and shrewd investors could gauge the direction of Indiana's development and buy out the land ahead of the leading edge of settlement, only to sell it again at a higher price when the first farmers arrived. This land-jobbing, or land speculation, had been something of an American obsession since colonial days. Everyone from George Washington down bought and sold land this way, looking for a profit, and land speculation was a key part of the Hoosier economy. Much of central and northern Indiana was in fact settled not by yeoman farmers who staked their claims directly with the federal government, but rather by investors who identified desirable future farmland, purchased that land, and then resold it to those yeoman farmers.[38]

Hand in hand with land speculating came, oddly enough, a burning hatred of land speculators as a blight and pestilence. Indiana's farmers liked to think of themselves as Jefferson's hardy and self-reliant pioneers who came by their wealth naturally and honestly, showing up on empty wilderness soil and improving it with the honest labor that was the backbone of the American Dream. That a cunning land speculator would arrive ahead of them, buy up the land, and then make a profit from their pursuit of that dream seemed lazy and vaguely dishonest. People labeled as speculators subsequently incurred the suspicion and wrath of their neighbors. Describing a land auction in central Indiana in 1824, a Hoosier noted wryly that "if a speculator makes a bid, or shows a disposition to take a settler's claim from him, he soon sees the whites of a score of eyes snapping at him, and at the first opportunity he crawfishes out of the crowd."[39]

On a purely business level, demonizing land speculators made little sense. They were essential investors and movers of capital, helping develop the state's embryonic economy. But it emphasizes an important point: when farmers moved to Indiana, they did not just bring with them the business practices of yeoman farming; they also brought a certain culture, a value system that tried to distinguish between proper and improper behavior, right and wrong ways of living. Those values were not always logical, but they were pervasive and powerful.

Indiana's value system extolled first and foremost the virtue and rewards of unrelenting manual labor. "Real" work was with the hands more than the head, supplemented by a strong, unyielding back and above all a willingness to persevere. The highest praise an Indiana farmer could earn from his neighbors was not that said farmer had gotten rich quick, made clever land deals, or sought high intellectual attainment; it was, rather, that he had worked long and hard and inexorably beat down the many obstacles presented by the state's harsh countryside. "At the time of his settlement here Indians were the principle inhabitants, and game and wild animals roamed through the forests," read a typical glowing tribute to one William Blue of Kosciusko County, but "after clearing a place on which to erect a rude log cabin he went bravely to work to clear his farm, and by much hard work and indomitable energy he developed it into a splendid farm" and became "one of the oldest and most respected of the pioneers now living."[40]

That label "pioneer" carried a heavy freight of value judgments about one's character. An Indiana pioneer was someone who built something from nothing and did so with moxie and stoic boldness. "The pioneers were wont to carry their rifles in their hands, as they visited from cabin to cabin," one early Indiana chronicler wrote, for "such were [their] surroundings." This requisite martial bravery applied not just to the farmers who constituted the state's majority, but also to anyone who wanted to settle and develop Indiana. "We not only need men whose hearts are imbued with grace, and whose minds are richly stored with human science," read a prospectus for a southern Indiana seminary, "but we need those, who possess *firm health and a vigorous constitution*—those in short, who are able '*to endure hardness as good soldiers*.'"[41]

Hoosiers liked to think of themselves as a tough bunch, "hardy, fearless and generally honest, but more or less reckless," as an Indiana circuit court judge put it.[42] They actually reveled in the tales of ravenous panthers and bears, Indian attacks, and the like as evidence of their indomitable spirit. They valued self-reliance, and some made their state's formal rejection of slavery a badge of honor in that regard, the early efforts to introduce slavery into the state notwithstanding. "Above all, [Indiana farmers] have carried into that vast field an honest love of labor," enthused one Indiana booster, "and in the very act of organizing their governments, they testified their willingness to exert and rely on their own energies, by prohibiting slavery forever, throughout all their limits."[43]

At the center of this Hoosier value system was religion and a vibrant Indiana church life. Insofar as Indiana possessed an infrastructure, it lay in the churches that dotted the landscape and the itinerant ministers who crisscrossed the state, battling all those traveling impediments to bring the word of God to their flock in the wilderness.

"Society is in a chaotic state," noted one early resident of the central Indiana town of Crawfordsville, "but the floating elements begin to indicate some definite formations. The Baptists talk of building a small house of worship. The Reverend Hackaliah Vredenburg, of the Methodist denomination, preached here a few Sabbaths ago, and took incipient steps for the organization of a church, while the Presbyterians think strongly of building a college north-west of town." If people gathered in any significant number for any length of time in any corner of Indiana, a church of some fashion soon followed.[44]

Not every Hoosier was given to churchgoing, however; in fact, some travelers found Indiana's residents to be shockingly bereft of morals and piety, given to gambling, fighting, and drinking in excess. "Their common language was that of profane songs, vulgar jokes and low ribaldry," sniffed an indignant traveler from the East.[45] But Indiana's farmers were more often than not God-fearing Christians of the severe Protestant variety—sober men and women who believed the Lord called on them to exchange bad language, strong drink, and much else in the way of earthly self-indulgence for glory in the hereafter. "Worship not the *world*," declaimed an Indiana Episcopal minister, "that absorbing love of its perishing gifts, that deep regard for [the world's] voice, which makes men so careless of the pleadings of conscience and the voice of God."[46]

Indiana ministers told their congregations that God expected of them those same values of self-discipline, self-reliance, and perseverance they needed to build a functioning farm in the wilderness: the "pioneer" life was the Christian life and vice versa. Those preachers who toiled in the deep woods alongside hardworking farmers were likewise doing good work. "When the rural minister . . . finds himself in the midst of a poor, but industrious and praying people, who are ready to go to the last inch in the service of God," declared one church leader, "he cannot, if he loves his Master's work, regret the obscurity and oblivion which covers him."[47]

Education was valued in Indiana as a twin offshoot of religious piety, for to know how to read was to have access to the Bible. Along with all those little wilderness churches were often little schoolhouses, or sometimes buildings that doubled as both, combining "book learning" with ministry in ways impossible to separate. Asked by a traveling minister whether his town possessed a church, an old man replied, "No . . . but we have a heap of preaching in the schoolhouse yonder. . . . Methodist, Baptist, Reformers, New Lights, United Brethren, Universalist, and Presbyterian. . . . It's all a mixed-up mess to me."[48]

But Indiana farmers' belief in the value of education had its limits. They wanted the basics of knowledge for themselves and their children, the better to understand God's words and plan, but not to the point that such knowledge became a distraction from the long hours of manual labor required to create and maintain a viable farm. A man who devoted too much time and energy to books and not enough time holding an ax or pushing a plow risked the perception that he was an idler, unwilling to do "real" work. One state legislator speaking of the need to educate Indiana farmers complained about the "too prevalent notion that education disqualifies a man for labor, or as it is generally termed 'makes him lazy.'"[49]

In any event, precious few books were available to a typical Indiana farmer; there were not even all that many newspapers, at least not in 1816. This would soon change. By the mid-1820s cheaper printing presses would fuel an explosion in the number of daily and weekly papers printed throughout America, to the point that even the smaller Indiana towns usually had at least one newspaper, often more.[50]

The increasing number of newspapers in turn fed a growing fascination with politics, in Indiana and nationwide. Nearly every newspaper carried a political affiliation, usually passionately so, and editors were deeply embedded in party politicking, debates, arguments, and often political controversy. Suffrage restrictions for adult white males had largely vanished throughout America by the time Indiana became a state, and Hoosiers followed this trend. Indiana's first constitution gave the vote to all white males twenty-one and over, and the state's political culture developed accordingly, with candidates appealing to the (white) common man, usually a farmer, and his concerns. This meant a lot of stump speeches at gatherings in remote corners of the state. An Indiana lawyer named Sandford Cox recalled attending a congressional election rally "in a little half-finished frame house" in Lafayette in 1828. Both candidates "made good speeches, considering their plight at the time—having laid out on the Wea plain the previous night, without shelter or supper, and not getting their ham, eggs and coffee until about ten o'clock the next day." Such rallies were the occasion for a rare break from the endless rounds of farming chores, and Cox recalled settlers coming from twenty miles away to attend the festivities, some by canoe down the Wabash River.[51]

It was an appropriately curious mix: the relative sophistication of democratic politics coupled with the primitiveness of a canoe ride down a wild Indiana river. When the Lincolns landed on the Ohio River's northern shore, they entered a state that was just such a set of contradictions writ large, with a big, diverse, and in many ways quite powerful and growing Hoosier population, at once exhilarating and terrifying, progressive in its free-soil ways and rejection of slavery, but in other ways disturbingly violent, its mismatched pieces of different peoples and cultures creating opportunities for all sorts of havoc. Yet for all its diversity, Indiana was at the same time developing a dominant set of values and customs, rooted in its agricultural economy, its powerful tradition of evangelical Protestantism, and its common-man political landscape. Thomas Lincoln and his family would more or less blend right in, becoming still another farm family trying to hack a living out of the unforgiving southern Indiana forest.

And that "gawky" kid standing by his older sister, parents, and cousin that cold day in 1816, staring at the approaching shore? He would embody much of early Indiana's culture as well. But he would also prove to be the exception to a great many rules.

ROOTS

Both Thomas and Nancy Lincoln possessed deep roots in America, with a lineage stretching well back into the seventeenth century. Tracing those roots is no simple task. Abraham Lincoln himself found his family history mysterious, fraught with "incertitude, and absolute darkness of names and dates," as one of his campaign biographers put it. "We have a vague tradition that my great-grand father went from Pennsylvania to Virginia," Lincoln wrote in 1848, "Further back than this, I have never heard any thing. . . . I know so little of our family history."[1]

His family was English in origin. The earliest reliable documentation shows Samuel Lincoln, a teenage weaver's apprentice, migrating from England to Massachusetts in 1637, where he and his wife, Martha, eventually raised a family of eleven children. One of those children, Mordecai, in turn raised another Mordecai, who raised John Lincoln, who then begat Abraham—the president's grandfather and namesake. In the process the Lincoln family line proved quite mobile, following a generally westward track from Massachusetts into New Jersey, Virginia, and Kentucky.[2]

These were what might have been described at the time as "plain folk," farmers and tradesmen, blacksmiths and millwrights— "undistinguished families," Abraham Lincoln later remembered. He could later claim with justification to have come from humble roots—a distinct political advantage—but taken as a whole the Lincoln lineage was not quite *that* humble. His grandfather Abraham, often referred to as Captain Lincoln because of his Revolutionary

War service, was a weaver and tanner by trade, and also a shrewd land investor. He had by the mid-eighteenth century managed to assemble a considerable amount of acreage—over five thousand acres, scattered in various parcels around Virginia.[3]

By the time Thomas Lincoln was born to Captain Abraham in 1778, the family was living in Virginia's Rockingham County. Following that long tradition of Lincolnian mobility, the captain removed his family in 1782 to the far western Virginia frontier—so far west in fact that it later became part of the new state of Kentucky.[4] The area in which they settled was disputed ground, and much like the Indiana frontier twenty years later, it was the scene of incessant conflict between whites and Native American tribes. In May 1786 these problems landed in the Lincolns' midst, with tragic consequences.

While constructing a fence on their farm, Captain Abraham and his sons were suddenly attacked by a small raiding party, probably Shawnee. A warrior concealed in the nearby brush shot and killed the captain, grabbed six-year-old Thomas by the trousers, and took off. Thomas's thirteen-year-old brother, Mordecai, ran inside the family cabin nearby, clambered into the loft with a gun, drew a bead on a silver half-moon pendant hanging from the Shawnee's neck—"the prettiest mark he held a rifle on," he later claimed—and fired. Mortally wounded, the man dropped Thomas and stumbled away. His body was found the next day at the end of a blood trail in the underbrush.[5]

Mordecai could never forget or forgive his father's death. He harbored a bitter hatred for Native Americans thereafter. It was said he sometimes assaulted and even killed Native Americans whom he happened upon, "when he could without it being known that he was the person that done the deed." Later in life he tracked down and murdered a Native American for no other reason than that the unfortunate man happened to be passing through his neighborhood. Mordecai left the body in a sinkhole, justifying the deed by telling friends that "the Indians had killed his farther [sic] and he was determined to have satisfaction."[6]

For Thomas, the death of his father imposed serious limitations on his future. Captain Lincoln was a fairly substantial landowner when he died, but following the old English custom of primogeniture, his land was awarded to eldest son Mordecai. Thomas inherited nothing. Formerly the son of a successful landowner and artisan, he would now be raised by a single mother, with the help of various local relatives and friends, in an age when this often meant penury and hardship.

Bathsheba Lincoln apparently had been present when her husband was killed; one story has her motioning Mordecai into the cabin as he climbed into the loft for a clear shot at his father's assailant. No doubt traumatized by the affair, Mrs. Lincoln removed her family to another area of Kentucky, in present-day Washington County south of Louisville. She does not seem to have remarried and lived in what her grandson Abraham later described as "very narrow circumstances" with Thomas and her other children.

When Thomas met Nancy Hanks, probably sometime in the early 1800s, her background was, if anything, more problematic than Thomas's and even today remains something of a mystery. Like Thomas, she was a native Virginian, and the Hanks family traced a similar line of settlement and resettlement on various farms in Pennsylvania and Virginia during the eighteenth century. Nancy herself was illegitimate, a fact of which her son was aware. During a buggy ride in 1850, Abraham Lincoln confided to his law partner, William Herndon, in a "sad and absorbed" manner: "[Nancy] was the illegitimate daughter of Lucy Hanks and a well-bred Virginia farmer," Herndon recalled Lincoln saying, along with Lincoln's belief that "his better nature and finer qualities came from this broad-minded, unknown Virginian."[7] Recent DNA evidence has established that Nancy was, in fact, born out of wedlock to Anne Lee Hanks.[8]

Whatever the truth of her origins, by the time she met Thomas, Nancy was a seamstress residing in the home of her uncle, Richard Berry, near Thomas Lincoln's farm. Exactly how and when they met, and the nature and circumstances of their courtship, are unknown. They were married in Berry's home in June 1806.

They eventually settled on a small farm in Hardin County, Kentucky, in an area called Knob Creek. There Thomas emulated his father by farming and trying to accumulate as much land as possible. But landownership in Kentucky was chancy business. The state was notorious for its sloppy paperwork and disorganized land claims system. Kentucky farmers were expected to hire their own surveyors or survey their land themselves, either of which might or might not result in accurate boundaries. The area in which Thomas lived was often a trackless, rolling landscape with confusing landmarks and all sorts of obstacles for surveyors trying to establish clear boundary lines, and he was surrounded by other farmers of a similar bent and background moving into the same general area and likewise trying to carve out little landholding empires.

Competition for good land was stiff. Still, Thomas had managed to accumulate about three hundred acres of land by 1810. And as his acreage grew, so too did his family. Sarah was born in 1807, Abraham in the dead of winter 1809. At some point Thomas and Nancy welcomed their third child into the world, a boy named Thomas after his father. But Thomas Jr. died while still a baby, from causes unknown, and was buried in Kentucky.[9]

By the time Abraham was five years old, Thomas was feeling the Kentucky ground growing shaky under his feet. He had become embroiled in a series of complex legal actions and business transactions regarding his land. In 1814 he lost a substantial amount of acreage in an area called Mill Creek because of a paperwork error. A year later he was one of nine local farmers sued by Philadelphia speculators trying to eject the farmers from land the speculators had previously purchased. Thomas was also hauled into court for an unpaid debt in 1813, suggesting he was short on cash.[10]

The Lincolns were clearly struggling, but they were not alone. Quite a few Kentucky farmers found themselves similarly situated in a precarious way, with a shaky legal hold on their land and facing dire consequences should they find themselves on the losing end of a court decision that might deprive them of their livelihood and maybe even the very roof over their families' heads. "Whoever purchases land [in Kentucky]," warned an anonymous observer in 1786, "is sure to purchase a lawsuit."[11]

Early nineteenth-century America was a merciless place in these circumstances, and living in a slave state like Kentucky posed even more difficulties. A struggling farmer in a free state could at least hope to get by with menial labor until he scraped enough money together to buy some new land and start over. But in Kentucky slaves were available for these tasks, and free workers could not easily compete. "White labour cannot live in competition with slave labour," noted journalist Frederick Law Olmstead, because "the holder of slave-labour controls the local market for labour, and the cost of slave-labour fixes the cost of everything which is produced by slave-labour."[12]

This is the essential context for Abraham Lincoln's later assertion that his father wanted to leave Kentucky "partly on account of slavery," taken by some to suggest that Thomas Lincoln was morally opposed to human bondage and passed this sentiment along to his future Great Emancipator son.[13] Perhaps Thomas was indeed morally opposed to slavery, and it is true that while in Kentucky he attended churches with antislavery ministers. But how much Thomas absorbed their values is impossible to know, and there is no record of Thomas expressing a moral opposition to slavery or any opinion regarding African Americans one way or another.[14]

But it is not difficult to imagine Thomas growing increasingly worried about his prospects in a slave state with shaky land titles, discussing the "what ifs" of an uncertain future with friends, relatives, and probably a worried wife. By 1815 he had lost a considerable amount of land and money in Kentucky's courts. Far from getting ahead and slowly building a little landholding empire like his father, Thomas was slipping backward.

A time-honored remedy beckoned, however, taken by who knows how many struggling American farmers fortunate enough to live in a growing country with a seemingly endless supply of unclaimed (at least by white farmers) land. Indiana was there, not so far away. Moving would not be easy, of course; it never was. But maintaining the status quo might be more difficult and risky, and picking up stakes and starting over was hardly an unfamiliar strategy. When he looked toward the Ohio River and a fresh start, Thomas was following what amounted to a family tradition.

He made at least one preliminary visit to Indiana before moving his family from Kentucky, possibly more, sometime in the spring or summer of 1816, when traveling was relatively easy. No one knows exactly where he went in Indiana or how long he stayed, but he does not seem to have ventured very far north of the Ohio River, scouting instead for available land that would not require him to move his family too deep into the wilderness. When he found a likely spot, he marked it off "by making blazes—brush heaps, etc. to make a location," as Dennis Hanks described it.[15] Neither Dennis nor any-one else seems to have accompanied Thomas on this scouting trip. When he returned, he and his family made their preparations for departure, and at some point Dennis agreed to help them with the move. Dennis was Nancy's cousin, the illegitimate son of Nancy's aunt, also named Nancy. "I went myself with them backwards and forwards—to Indiana—and back to Kentucky," Hanks later wrote. Thomas probably wanted Dennis along to help with some of the more cumbersome tasks involving heavy lifting that would have proven difficult for one man.

Hanks was the primary eyewitness to what life was like for himself and the Lincolns during those first days in Indiana. His account is not always reliable; by the time he was interviewed in 1865, he was an old man trying to recall events that had occurred nearly fifty years previously, and he sometimes became confused regarding dates and other details. He was "fast failing in body and mind" by this point, according to one observer. But he was able to convey at least the general tenor of those difficult times in the fall and winter of 1816–17.[16]

When they arrived at Thompson's Ferry on the Ohio River's north-ern shore, they began working their way into the interior, probably aiming for the general area Thomas had earlier explored, known lo-cally as Little Pigeon Creek, part of what would in 1818 become Spen-cer County. Their route seems to have generally followed a stream called the North Fork until one branch became Little Pigeon Creek, which in turn led them to a spring that would become a vital source of fresh water for the new Lincoln farm.[17]

The going was slow, encumbered as they were with livestock, furniture, and other belongings, and with no roads, Thomas had to "cut his way to his farm with the axe felling the forest as he went," remembered a friend. It took them an entire day to work their way into the interior from the ferry to the land Thomas had earlier marked out with his brush piles.[18]

Their first and most urgent task was to create some kind of shelter. They constructed what amounted to a rough lean-to, described by Hanks as "a little two-face camp open in front, serving a momentary purpose." During their second day in this ramshackle affair, Abraham spotted a flock of wild turkeys nearby. Thomas (and probably Dennis) was away from the site at the time, and Abraham was too little to load a gun, so Nancy did it for him. "Abe poked the gun through the crack of the camp," Hanks remembered, "and accidentally killed one, which he brought to the camp house."[19]

With winter approaching, Thomas could not very well rely on his "little two-face camp," so he and Dennis quickly went to work building something more permanent. Within a day they had erected a tiny log cabin, so small that it barely allowed the adults to stand erect. Like the lean-to, this was "a temporary affair," though in the end it was made to last the entire winter. It is not hard to imagine how almost insufferably crowded that little log cabin must have been for a family of five, especially on cold winter days when no one could venture outdoors. Furniture was crude, "split with mawl and wedges out of large logs and dressed off with the broad axe," according to Hanks. Sleeping arrangements must likewise have been tight, and when lighting a fire was necessary (Hanks makes no mention of a fireplace or chimney, though surely they eventually added some such arrangement for warmth and cooking), the air inside would have quickly acquired a smoky acridness.[20]

With no crop yet planted, the family depended primarily on hunting to carry them through that first winter. "We always hunted," Dennis remembered, "it made no difference what came for we more or less depended upon it for a living—nay for life." Fortunately the area was teeming with animals. "We did not have to go more than four or five hundred yards to kill deer, turkeys and other wild game," Dennis said. They also discovered an abundance of "bee trees" and wild honey. A mill was available for grinding cornmeal, but it was seventeen miles away on the river and was "a poor concern." Still, Hanks believed, it was "a God Send."[21]

Winter was fast approaching as they began to settle in and adjust to their new surroundings. It was far too late in the season to begin any serious attempt at planting. They occupied themselves with simply clearing an area around the cabin by felling trees and cutting away the underbrush. Abraham could not yet contribute much in the way of severe manual labor. "Abe could do little jobs," Hanks recalled, "such as carry water, go to the springs, branches, etc."[22]

The area was very remote, but not empty. Hanks later claimed that "Indians . . . were plenty," though he did not mention any specific encounters, nor did Abraham in his later reminiscences of his childhood. Hanks also said, "We had no trouble with the Indians in Indiana, [because] they soon left and [traveled] westward."[23] There were also neighboring farms scattered about here and there on similar plots of land. The Grigsby family, for example, occupied a farm nearby, as did the Romines and the Richardsons. Hanks later estimated that about twenty people were living in the immediate area, but he may well have been exaggerating the Lincolns' isolation, for it seems that several reasonably large families lived nearby, and the area that would shortly be designated Spencer County was rapidly filling with farmers.[24]

The area had no real towns or even villages. Eventually Gentryville, about a mile and a half from the Lincoln farm, was established as the closest village in the immediate vicinity when James Gentry moved the little collection of goods he had been selling on his farm to a makeshift general store, which eventually became the nucleus of the town bearing his name. But when the Lincolns arrived in 1816, Gentryville barely existed, and the Little Pigeon Creek area had nothing else much resembling a town.[25]

When spring came, the Lincolns began the laborious process of planting their first crop, by no means a simple operation. Hanks later recalled that they had managed by this point to clear about six acres for planting, an impressive achievement given the weather and other obstacles.[26] But *clear* was a relative term. What exactly did it mean to clear a plot of south Indiana farmland in an age when farmers relied on only their own strong backs and a few simple tools?

Thomas and his family would have begun the process of clear-ing any given patch of land by first going after the thick, tangled underbrush, a mass of grass, weeds, thorns, and small bushes of every variety—persimmon, paw-paw, sassafras, redbud—that cov-ered the ground and made planting and sometimes even walking almost impossible. Indiana farmland was notorious for this. "It is said to be very difficult to cultivate land in Indiana, on account of the extremely vigorous vegetation," noted a European visitor. Even surveying the land could be difficult. "I have frequently heard Mr. Fisher [a local land surveyor] say that the men had to precede him and clear away the underbrush so he could get a sight through his instrument," remembered one Indiana man.[27]

Farmers sometimes used fire to rid their land of brush, though this was naturally a risky operation, should the fire spread out of control; on the other hand, farmers believed the scorched soil yielded a better harvest.[28] Others preferred simply wading into the brush and cutting it down with knives or scythes or ripping it out by hand, operations sometimes called "grubbing," work to which all three of the youngsters—Dennis, Sarah, and Abraham—could contribute.

This would have been sweaty, hard work, but in fact it was the relatively easy part of the clearing operation. Next they had to remove the trees, and these were by far the biggest challenge Hoosier farm-ers faced. Even more than its underbrush, Indiana was known for its nearly impenetrable tree growth: oak, poplar, ash, maple, locust, and gum, hardwoods and soft, large and small, trees with odd local nicknames such as "spindle tree" or the "toothache tree," and of greater or lesser value for firewood, building materials, or crafts. One nineteenth-century expert estimated that Indiana was home to over one hundred different species of trees. They were particularly dense in the southern region, where the Lincolns were making their home.[29]

Felling one of these trees—say, a forty-foot oak—was a difficult operation. Farmers needed to know how to properly estimate when a half-chopped tree would begin to fall and especially where it would land, avoiding their cabins or themselves. Once felled, it then had to be removed. After cutting it into somewhat smaller pieces, the Lin-colns, possibly with the help of neighbors, would have engaged in the backbreaking work of "log-rolling." This involved loading the pieces of trunk and larger branches onto "handspikes," six-foot-long poles flattened a bit at one end, and then manhandling the timber away from the field to be either burned or chopped into still smaller pieces.[30]

Finally, they had to deal with the stumps. Thomas's long-term goal was to remove the stumps, along with as much of the root systems as possible. But stump removal was, if anything, more difficult than cutting away the tree, given that the trees generally produced root systems as deep as their branches were high. Some farmers tried to burn the stumps; others used black powder to blast them away. One approach involved using a twenty-foot wooden pole, a stout log chain, and a pair of oxen to pry the stump out of the ground; this was described by one farmer as "a very simple and economic process." Or the Lincolns might have preferred a somewhat more complicated version of the same basic idea, whereby a lever was attached to a framework of boards with a hook at one end that curled under the stump and slowly pried it loose, again by means of oxen or some other animal or muscular power.[31]

Thomas may well have forgone stump removal altogether, at least in spring of 1817. He needed to get his crops planted, and soon; the quicker he cleared the land, the more he could plow and plant, and consume and sell. His first crop was critical: many an American farmer had been ruined by planting too little or too late in the harvest season. There was no margin of error, at least not yet. In future years Thomas could count on setting a little product and even a little money aside, hedging his bets against bad weather, insects, and any of a number of calamities. But in 1817 he would have had little or nothing in reserve.[32]

So Thomas likely decided to go at the trees in a short-term fashion. He, Dennis, and Abraham, and possibly a helpful neighbor or two, would have cleared much of the underbrush and smaller trees, and then "girdled" the larger ones, cutting a strip several inches wide completely around the base of the tree, through the bark and into the wood, thereby ensuring the tree's eventual death an estimated two or three seasons later, when the decay would be far enough along to allow felling the trunk.[33]

Or they might have "deadened" the timber in other ways. "All the trees under eighteen or twenty inches in diameter were then cut down," recalled a Hoosier pioneer, "and large brush heaps made around all the rest. The brush, when dry, were burned, scorching the trees some fifteen or twenty feet high, and killing them sooner than if they had been girdled with an axe."[34] Larger roots protruding from the ground also required removal, which could be accomplished by wielding mattocks, axlike tools with dual blades, to chip away at whatever was showing above the dirt.[35]

Abraham would have been squarely in the middle of these various clearing operations. If he was not actually felling giant trees with an ax, then he was surely involved in slicing the smaller branches, helping with handspike loads of logs, sweeping away chunks of dead and burned brush to level the field, or possibly monitoring the fires—if Thomas chose to employ that method—to ensure they did not burn out of control.

Once the trees and roots were at least somewhat cleared in this fashion, they addressed another obstacle to plowing. The soil in Indiana tended to be on the rocky side, and those rocks needed to be cleared away, lest they break a plow or cause a furrow to go awry. Large rocks would have been within the purview of Thomas, Dennis, and whatever draft animals they owned or borrowed, lashing the rock with a stout chain and ripping them loose in much the same manner as a tree stump. The smaller rocks probably fell to Abraham and Sarah, who would have pried them loose with sticks or their bare hands.

Nancy may well have also loaned a hand in the rock removal operation and perhaps other clearing tasks as well. In farming America of 1817, the lines between "men's work" and "women's work," while real, were blurred by necessity. Often enough mothers joined their children in the farm chores requiring lighter physical labor, and it is worth noting that, if she did step out into the fields, Nancy would have done so in addition to her other tasks: laundry, food preparation, general cleanliness, and childcare.[36]

Once the ground was sufficiently cleared, she may even have helped Thomas with the actual plowing of the fields, along with the children. Most frontier children learned to operate a plow at an early age, though it was a physically demanding task, made all the more so by the primitive plow designs that were available to farmers in 1817. The steel plow was still decades in the future (invented by John Deere in 1837), and even plows constructed of iron were somewhat rare, though plows with iron points or the moldboard sheathed in iron were fairly common. There was no standardized design, and everyone had a different idea regarding the ideal shape and size of the point, the moldboard, the optimum length of the handles, and the like. Given his relative lack of money and resources, Thomas Lincoln's plow was almost certainly a simple wooden affair, probably not much more than a wooden stick thrust into the earth, with handles and leather reins for whatever draft animals he employed, or possibly shouldered himself. It may have had some ironwork fashioned by a local blacksmith, but likely no wheel or other mechanism to assist in keeping the furrow straight.[37]

We have no reliable record concerning what sort of draft animal Thomas employed for that first crop. Oxen were the preferred animals, given their size and sturdiness. But they were also expensive to purchase and maintain, and there is no indication that Thomas owned oxen at this point in his life. He did bring at least two horses with him on that first flatboat trip across the Ohio, so it is likely that he and his family hitched a horse to his plow.[38]

We also have no direct record regarding what Thomas chose to plant in the newly cleared ground; in all likelihood it was a species of corn called "gourd seed," a tall, sturdy variety well suited to the climate. Indiana farmers of the day tended to plant corn for their first cash crop; wheat was more profitable, but Indiana's soil was too rich in nutrients and vegetable matter to support a wheat crop until successive corn crops had depleted the soil. But a good portion of any given Indiana farm would have been devoted to planting various foodstuffs for the family's own consumption, anything from potatoes to squash, beans, tomatoes, sugar peas, cucumbers, cabbages, and so forth. Thomas may well have also planted a bit of tobacco, as did many other Hoosier farmers with southern connections; he had done so in Kentucky.[39]

To the modern eye, the Lincoln farm that first spring would have seemed like a veritable moonscape of scattered stumps, "deadened" tree trunks, perhaps a leftover charred pile of brush here and there, the land pockmarked with holes great and small where rocks had been excavated, scored by somewhat erratic furrows, and peppered with the little hills of dirt each containing four or five corn seeds—a backup system in case some of the seeds failed to sprout or were carried away by birds and other animals.[40] This was hardly the stuff of Jefferson's romantic yeoman farming paradise. The place would have exuded a half-finished air, all rough edges and rawness, the product of endless hours of hard manual labor.

All this work would have been exhausting and the source of probably more than a few injuries and mishaps. Apparently no one was seriously hurt on the Lincoln farm that first spring; at least, no record exists of broken bones or anything of that sort. Doctors were few and far between; Dennis claimed that the nearest doctor was thirty-five miles away.[41] But surely they all suffered their share of blisters, scrapes, cuts, and bruises. These injuries generally fell within Nancy's purview; and having spent her entire life on such farms and in such circumstances, she would have possessed a store of knowledge regarding how best to deal with them. Blisters could be treated with various types of bark, natural ointments, or lard. Bruises were thought to be best treated with bacon fat, butter mixed with a bit of oatmeal, or sometimes a poultice made from tobacco leaves. Any kind of puncture wound—from a nail or sharp stick, for example—Nancy would have treated with turpentine or possibly a mustard or potato poultice, keeping a careful watch for the first signs of infection or lockjaw, which could prove serious or even fatal. Nancy may have also followed a common practice among Indiana farmwives in creating a small store of medicinal compounds, herbs, and plants: calomel, mint, senna, and local varieties of horehound and poke root, useful for treating a range of ailments from sore muscles to indigestion.[42]

The family would have had little time for much in the way of leisure during that first spring, when everything was so new and chancy. Very likely everyone labored from sunup to sundown with no letup, save for services on Sunday at the nearby Little Pigeon

Creek Baptist Church—not a "leisure" activity, exactly, but at least a welcome respite from the fields. Hunting was another diversion. "We all hunted pretty much all the time," Dennis recalled, "especially so when we got tired of work—which was very often."[43]

By the following fall, Thomas was preparing to reap his first corn harvest in Indiana. He and his family had now been Hoosiers for almost a year. They had put down a new set of roots, with the hope and promise of better, more settled days to come.

MOTHERS

By the time of their second harvest in the fall of 1818, the Lincolns were well settled into their little corner of Indiana. They had slowly but steadily expanded the acreage under cultivation, growing corn and winter wheat as foundational crops, accompanied by whatever varieties of foodstuffs they chose for their own dinner table. Just west of their log cabin lay a large garden for that purpose, though they would also have planted intertillage crops: pumpkins interspersed between the corn hills, possibly, or any of a variety of different types of beans.[1]

The pumpkins were not just for human consumption; they also made excellent fodder for the Lincolns' growing collection of livestock. Eventually the family constructed both a smokehouse and a chicken house, with the privy in between, and acquired "the usual domestic animals, known to civilization," as Dennis put it. This included a cow and at least one ox, which surely made plowing season function a bit more smoothly. They also added hogs—purchased in Kentucky, then driven to the farm—and continued to supplement their diet with whatever wild animals they could hunt in the surrounding countryside.[2]

Small Indiana farms managed, despite their size and remoteness, to assemble an impressive variety of foods. Serious nutritional information was largely nonexistent in the early nineteenth century, but farmers like Thomas and Nancy understood, by instinct and experience, the importance of a daily diet rich in diverse vegetables, fruits, and dairy and meat products—fuel for all those long days of heavy physical labor. Common stereotypes of the time had poor "white trash" frontier farmers barely scraping by on corn, beans, and wild game, supplemented by liberal amounts of homemade alcohol of one sort or another. "The height of their ambition," sniffed one observer, "is to get an old horse and a pair of wheels, with corn-husk collars and rope reins, by which they may obtain sufficient money to buy a quart of whiskey."[3]

The truth was much different. The typical small farm was actually a complex operation, with quite a few moving parts and requiring Thomas Lincoln to continually exercise fairly sophisticated expertise and decision-making skills. He could in no reasonable sense have been described as either dull-witted or lazy; his farm allowed him no such luxury. As head of the family, it was he who made the daily decisions, great and small, that shaped his Indiana farm—everything from cultivation and harvest techniques to the optimal location for the smokehouse.

The family faced other challenges as well, chief among them a reliable source of water. Thomas "wanted water badly," according to Dennis Hanks. He had tried to dig a well, but the result was a "miserable article" that produced a very poor quality of water. At one point a man appeared in the area who claimed to be able to locate water with a divining rod—for the sum of $5. This would have been a considerable amount of money for a farmer like Thomas, who did not place much trust in the "Yankee" stranger and ran him off.[4] So they continued to rely on water hand-carried from a spring that was down a hill to the west of the cabin. The water was important more for bathing and doing laundry than for drinking, for everyone knew that water was often not to be trusted. Instead, the Lincolns relied primarily on their milk cow and probably a bit of spirits.[5]

Milking the family cow, hauling water uphill from the spring, gathering chicken eggs, and tending the family garden patch all were chores done by the children and by Nancy. Her tasks probably seemed endless. One neighbor described her as a "laboring woman"; she was a rather unobtrusive and patient sort, even in the face of the daily hardships posed by what must have been a tough life—"meek, quiet and amiable" was how Dennis described her, saying he "never knew her to be out of temper." Others agreed; "her nature was kindness— mildness [and] tenderness," thought one neighbor. Not physically robust, Nancy nevertheless held up well under the stress, for there is no record of her having fallen ill during those most difficult first months in Indiana. She also gave everyone around her the impression of being intellectually inclined, a thoughtful and mentally bright person, "keen [and] shrewd," and gifted with an excellent memory.[6]

Her activities as wife and mother involved expertise and skills that rivaled or surpassed those of her husband. In the fall she probably would have begun to lay in a store of preserved and pickled vegetables and fruits to see the family through the winter, when they might otherwise have been reduced to the stereotypical "white trash" fare of corn pone, beans, and dried pork for their daily meals. Abraham might have helped his mother fill a tub with vinegar to begin the pickling process, followed by a bushel or two of cucumbers, possibly mixed with hominy to create a relish. She needed to know how to carry out this process, properly store the finished product for future use, and manage her supply for the long winter, as well as how to cultivate batches of sage and other herbs to flavor the meats that Thomas preserved in the smokehouse; how to grow peppers, considered desirable not only for their flavor but also as a preventive for colds, dysentery, and other ailments; and what to do with the potatoes, turnips, radishes, and other root vegetables that were common on Indiana farms of the day.[7]

Additionally, Nancy was responsible for the family's weaving duties. She was working as a seamstress when Thomas met her back in Kentucky, so she possessed expertise in working with cloth. Like most Indiana farmers, Thomas put in a small patch of flax—probably around a quarter acre—to provide the raw material for clothing, bed linen, and other household textiles. Flax was considered stronger than cotton and better able to withstand the daily wear and tear of farmwork. Still, Nancy was surely kept constantly occupied mending or replacing damaged clothing. She performed her weaving duties in a "little shed," possibly because of a lack of space in the main cabin.[8]

The farm was a busy beehive of production, with Nancy at its center. On any given day Abraham might have seen his mother hanging strings of red peppers along the wall to dry; separating out the fibers from the stems of flax plants preparatory to making a shirt or a bedsheet (and likely helping her in that process, as "swingling" the flax was a task often assigned to young boys); seasoning freshly slaughtered venison or other recently acquired game for the evening meal; fashioning homemade candles called "sluts," made by wrapping linen around a wooden dowel, which was then doused in tallow; hanging freshly laundered clothing and bedding on pegs; and trying to stay ahead of what was surely a constant wave of dirt, grass, weeds, mud, insects—whatever nature and her hardworking family might drag across the threshold of that tiny cabin.[9]

All this required knowledge and ability. Nancy Lincoln was not merely a drudge, toiling mindlessly away. Many of her jobs as a "laboring woman" did indeed call for heavy physical work, but she was also a manager, skilled at a variety of tasks and carrying in her head a storehouse of information and lore. That she was quiet and unassuming, and that her labors probably went largely unnoticed and unheralded by the men around her—as was the case with most women in most such situations in early America—rendered her no less important or vital to the everyday life of the Lincoln family farm. "The housewife and her operations are the great regulator of the operations of the farm," noted one nineteenth-century writer, and "however judiciously and economically the plans for the operations of the farm may be laid, if a man and his wife do not harmonize, most completely, in prosecuting their labors, he had better at once dispose of his farm."[10]

In addition to being a vital cog in the farm's machinery, Nancy was also the mother of two children. By the fall of 1818 she was thirty-three years old—middle-aged by that day's standards and past the point when she might reasonably have been expected to bear any more children, nor did she do so.[11] Sarah and Abraham were eleven and nine, respectively, old enough to largely take care of themselves and to be of useful service in the daily farm chores. Nancy's life was therefore at least somewhat easier than if she had to care for an infant or younger children.

Yet Sarah and Abraham still required mothering, which by this point was largely a matter of teaching. Nancy was probably beginning to show her young daughter how to spin and sew, the basics of food preparation and gardening, housekeeping and general cleanliness, and the other tasks Sarah would someday be expected to perform when she became a wife and mother. Unfortunately, there is no direct primary source evidence regarding Nancy's relationship with her daughter, so we can only surmise that she followed the practices common to Indiana farm mothers of the day, many of whom thought it was a good idea to educate daughters as well as sons in at least the basics of agriculture and maintaining a properly functioning farm household. "I think farmers' daughters should be well educated," mused one writer, "agriculture as a science being made honorable and the young misses in their teens not wholly neglecting or despising it."[12]

As for Abraham, we have only glimpses of his relationship with his mother—a few tiny shards of the elderly Dennis Hanks's memory when he recalled life on the Lincoln farm many years later. Dennis returned to Kentucky after helping the Lincolns with their initial ferry crossing and settlement, but he soon came back to Little Pigeon Creek, accompanying Nancy's uncle Thomas Sparrow and his wife, Elizabeth, who occupied what one neighbor later referred to as the "Lincolns' old camp," meaning perhaps the site where Thomas had first pitched the lean-to "two-face camp."[13]

Dennis spent much of his time with his nearby Lincoln relatives, and he remembered a little incident in which Abraham interrupted his mother's weaving with the question "Who was the father of Zebedee's children?" and then ran off with a laugh when his mother saw the joke, remarking playfully to her son, "Get out of here, you nasty little pup you." Dennis also recalled Nancy reading to her son and daughter, using both a copy of "Webster's old spelling book" and the family Bible. "Lincoln's mother learned him to read the Bible," Hanks recalled, to "study it and the stories in it and all that was moraly [*sic*] and affectionate in it, repeating it to Abe and his sister when very young."[14] He also claimed to have "taught Abe to write with a buzzards quillen [*sic*] which I killed with a rifle and having made a pen." Possibly it was necessary for him to do so because

Nancy may not have been able to write; a deed dating back to the Lincolns' Kentucky days in 1814 bears only an *X* for her signature.[15]

Perhaps while she was growing up in Kentucky, it was thought that Nancy needed to be able only to read the Bible so that she could someday provide her children with proper moral instruction and nothing more. By the early nineteenth century this was increasingly seen as the province of mothers, who were supposed to be uniquely equipped for the task. American mothers had a moral and civic duty to properly educate their children, especially their sons, in basic values, an idea championed by many of the nation's intellectual elites since the Revolution. Modern scholars have termed this "republican motherhood": a set of principles proposed by writers, educators, and political leaders of the early American era holding that mothers had a civic duty to properly educate their children in sound republican values, lest the fragile new experiment in American democracy fail.[16]

Republican motherhood was generally championed by white middle- and upper-class elites. But the early United States was a nation composed mostly of farmers like the Lincolns, and there was a certain politics of farmwifery, in which the Nancy Lincolns of America were to act as the guardians and transmitters of the young nation's moral and civic character in backwoods log cabins as well as the more respectable and urbane town and city homes. "We must look still to farmers' wives, who are blessed with children, for the men of strong frames, of iron nerves and heroic hearts, to accomplish our nation's destiny," argued one writer."[17]

How much any of this trickled down into rural southern Indiana is difficult to say. Even if Nancy and Thomas Lincoln were aware of these new cultural notions concerning Nancy's ideal role as a "republican" mother, the very rawness of their life would likely not have allowed her the luxury of acting on those ideals. We generally know very little about what sort of atmosphere she tried to create as a mother and a wife in her home, or even whether she was able to put much thought into the matter at all. It may well have been that, even after nearly two years in Indiana, she still thought largely in terms of simple survival on a day-to-day basis for her family and herself.

A careful reading of the sparse record Abraham left behind suggests as much. When he mentioned his mother—which was not very often—he did so within the context of his own extremely humble and limited roots, and the primitive circumstances of their early Indiana life. In his 1860 campaign autobiography, Lincoln's brief reference to Nancy is bracketed by vivid descriptions of Indiana's "unbroken forest," his lack of a formal education, and the broadly unintellectual environment within which he grew to manhood, suggesting that he, perhaps unwittingly, tended to associate his mother's memory with the wilderness and frontier rusticity, more so perhaps than anything else.[18]

Yet Dennis Hanks, however dim and sometimes untrustworthy his memory might have been, also gives us a small glimpse into something more than a life of bare subsistence. It is striking that of all the incidents he might have recalled years later regarding Nancy as a mother, those that stuck with him involved a joke about the Bible and a memory of Nancy reading and telling stories—poignant little images of teaching, not just scraping by. Nancy may not have been an ideal or intellectually sophisticated "republican mother," but in her own way, and with the limited tools given to her by circumstances and her humble upbringing, she endeavored to create in the Lincoln log cabin something resembling the early nineteenth-century ideal of a home in which to raise and educate young children.

Much of the same dynamic affected Nancy's role as Thomas's wife. Early nineteenth-century American marriages were in a transitional state, between older colonial ideas regarding husbands and wives as essentially reciprocal laborers who together worked toward creating a functioning family household or farm and newer, post-Revolution ideas holding that wives should be seen more as nurturers than as laborers. Husbands "worked" and wives provided a domestic place of respite when that work was done—or such was society's ideal, for the emerging middle class and perhaps others as well. A wife like Nancy Lincoln should from this point of view use her innate feminine virtues to create in the Lincoln home a safe, peaceful domestic atmosphere.[19]

But as with "republican motherhood," we do not know if these ideas regarding domesticity may be realistically applied to the Lincolns' Indiana home. It is also hard to tell whether Thomas expected as much from his wife or more generally just what sort of wife Nancy may have been. Just as the historical record is nearly silent regarding her mothering experiences, so too do we lack information regarding the couple's relationship and whether their marriage was fundamentally happy or strained. Nancy "never opposed her Husband in any thing, [and] was satisfied with what suited him," remembered a cousin, Augustus Chapman. The absence of any eyewitness testimony claiming otherwise would seem to suggest they were at least content with one another.[20]

Nancy, Thomas, and their children were far from isolated. The sometimes bewildering tangle of Kentucky relations had given the Lincolns their nearest neighbors, Elizabeth and Thomas Sparrow. The Sparrows still occupied the "two-face camp" nearby, along with Dennis Hanks and the nine-year old Sophia Hanks, one of the six illegitimate children of Nancy's sister, Sarah.[21] The Lincolns built relations with other farm families in the area as well. The Grigsbys lived nearby, Reuben and Nancy, with their ten children ranging from two to twenty-one years of age. They were, like the Lincolns, from Kentucky. Nathaniel Grigsby was two years younger than Abraham; the two boys would become good friends. Aaron Grigsby, age seventeen in 1818, eventually married Abraham's sister, Sarah.[22] Peter and Nancy Brooner were also recent Kentucky emigrants, of German descent. Peter was "a hardy, resolute man" and enjoyed a reputation as an accomplished bear hunter. He and Nancy often spoke German rather than English in their home. William Wood lived with his wife and four children on a hill north of the Lincoln farm. Wood hired Thomas to do quite a bit of carpentry work on his farm.[23]

For Nancy these neighborly connections were particularly important; American farm women of the time typically formed close-knit networks of mutual support, swapping everything from cloth to seeds, herbal lore, and childcare. Nancy was remembered as "charitable and affectionate," a good neighbor willing to come to others' aid when necessary. It was an admirable quality, but in the end it would cost her dearly.[24]

Sometime in the early fall the Sparrows fell ill, with uncontrollable shaking, severe thirst, a loss of appetite, general fatigue, and severe stomach cramps and vomiting. At the same time, Nancy Brooner became ill with much the same symptoms. The cramps and vomiting would have grown steadily worse, robbing them still further of energy and producing debilitating aches and fatigue. Visitors to their cabins might also have noted a peculiar smell and a foulness of breath among the inhabitants.

The Sparrows and Nancy Brooner were suffering from what was known as the "milk sickness," caused when cows ingested a local plant called white snakeroot. In the daisy family, white snakeroot may have seemed innocuous enough, but it contained tremetol, a chemical that turned the cow's milk into a deadly poison. The poison could even infect the cow's body. "Many instances of death among horned cattle have occurred in this county," noted a Tennessee man, "and dogs feeding upon their dead carcasses have become diseased, and some have died."[25]

Milk sickness was a much-feared, usually fatal scourge among settlers in Indiana and other parts of the American Midwest. No one in the early nineteenth century understood the connection among the white snakeroot plant, cow milk, and the disease; they saw that it seemed to occur immediately after the victim had consumed milk, but they had no idea why. White snakeroot did not normally grow in the eastern parts of the United States, so migrants moving west had no previous experience with the plant nor understanding of how dangerous it might be. They simply knew that frontier communities could and sometimes did become stricken, and the result was often widespread panic. There were theories that the poison originated from minerals, cold weather, and even tainted air. An outbreak could devastate an area beyond the actual deaths it involved. "Its prevalence often served as a cause to disband a community, and compel the inhabitants to seek a location which enjoyed immunity from its occurrence," noted one physician of the time.[26]

Nancy came to the aid of the Sparrows and Nancy Brooner, all three of whom died of the disease, along with one of Brooner children, and at some point Nancy ingested the poison.[27] Possibly she drank tainted milk, though one imagines she would have avoided drinking the very product her dying neighbors had consumed. But tremetol could taint any sort of dairy product—cheese, butter, cream—or beef, and Nancy would have had no way of identifying its presence, as it lacked taste and odor.[28]

She lingered for quite a while after initially falling ill—"struggled on day by day," Dennis recalled—in what must have been excruciating pain, the vomiting and retching produced by milk sickness being so persistent and violent that some referred to it as the "puking disease." The fatigue and wracking pain soon had Nancy bedridden, probably in that same tiny cabin Thomas had so hastily constructed during their first Indiana winter. Sympathetic neighbors came and went; William Wood later remembered sitting up with Nancy all night.[29]

By the time a week had passed, Hanks said, "she knew she was going to die." He remembered her calling Abraham and Sarah to her bedside, where she "told them to be good and kind to their father." On October 5, 1818, she passed away. Her body and Nancy Brooner's were hauled on makeshift sleds to a hill south of the Lincoln farm and buried under a grove of persimmon trees. After they had both shoveled dirt over their wives' graves, Peter Brooner, who had escaped the disease along with his sons Henry and Allen, offered his hand to Thomas. "We are brothers now," Peter said.[30]

"They were brothers in the same kind of sorrow," as Henry Brooner put it.[31] At the age of forty, Thomas now found himself a widower. It was a daunting prospect. The farm was still relatively new, requiring constant attention. At the same time, Thomas's little family had suddenly and of necessity expanded. Dennis Hanks would now reside permanently at Little Pigeon Creek with the Lincolns; a strapping youth nearly grown to manhood, he would be of considerable help, as would Abraham. The household duties now fell to young Sarah, and the Sparrows' niece Sophia, apparently having nowhere else to go, also moved in with the Lincolns.[32] Thomas therefore had in his care three children and one adolescent, ranging from nine to nineteen years old.

No direct record exists of what daily life was like on the Lincoln farm in the months immediately after Nancy's passing. Probably an air of sadness pervaded the little farm—that, and an air of squalor as well. "Abe and his sister did some work" while their mother lay dying, noted Dennis, but mostly "errand[s] and light work." With Nancy gone, the place required far more than "light work," and it probably became something close to uninhabitable. Thomas, Dennis, and Abraham would have been busy plowing, planting, and harvesting into the spring and summer, leaving Sarah and Sophia to manage the household duties in the cabin as best they could. It is highly unlikely they were equal to the task.[33]

Five people now resided in a tiny cabin with barely enough head-room to stand erect. Trying to alleviate the crowding—and perhaps with an eye toward accommodating a new wife for Thomas at some point in the near future—Thomas and Dennis began work on a better dwelling, "our new grand old log cabin," Dennis called it, probably the dwelling they occupied during the rest of their time in Indiana. When finished, the new cabin measured eighteen by twenty feet and was high enough to sport a loft where the family slept, reached by pegs anchored into one wall, "the pegs creaking and screeching as we went," remembered Dennis. While it must have been a significant improvement, the new cabin was not so very "grand," sporting a dirt floor, a single door, and only one window, with no glass.[34]

Sometime during the second half of 1819—late summer or possibly early fall—Thomas left Dennis in charge and headed for Kentucky. He was aiming for home, he may well have thought, returning to the Bluegrass State, which was not only his point of origin but also that of most of his Indiana neighbors. He knew Kentucky, he knew its people—and he knew he could quickly find a wife there. Thomas also knew who that wife would be.[35]

He had known Sarah Bush for a long time. Nine years younger than Thomas, Sarah was a Kentucky native from Elizabethtown, not far from where he had grown up. Physically she was quite different from Nancy, tall with "bluish large gray eyes." She was known as a very neat, even fastidious young woman who wore her hair in curls and paid attention to fashion.[36] Her background was also differ-ent from Nancy's. Sarah's father was a successful landowner with over two thousand acres to his name, and she had grown up in a large family with eight siblings, mostly brothers. She probably first met Thomas through his friendship with her brother Isaac and also perhaps via Thomas's acquaintance with her father, who captained a local slave patrol in which Thomas served.[37]

Local and family tradition held that Thomas Lincoln was one of Sarah's early suitors, but that he married Nancy after Sarah instead chose another man named Daniel Johnston. She may well have come to rue the choice, for following their marriage, Johnston struggled mightily to make a living, for reasons that are not entirely clear. They lost the five-hundred-acre farm Sarah brought with her as a dowry into the marriage and were unable to pay their taxes by 1806. Daniel was also sued for an unpaid debt four years later; he lost the case but was too broke to satisfy the judgment. He and Sarah were nearly penniless by 1814, when he accepted a job as county jailer. Sarah provided cleanup duties and prisoners' meals—a hard life, made still harder when Johnston died from cholera in 1816, after which she took up life as a "poor woman but of spotless character," residing still in Elizabethtown.[38]

Thomas seems to have known about Johnston's death, which occurred while the Lincolns still resided in Kentucky; and he knew exactly what he was after when he returned to Kentucky three years later, making what one friend called "a flying trip to Kentucky" to ask for Sarah's hand. He came right to the point. "In a plain Straight forward Manner [he] told her that they knew each other from child hood, that he had no wife and she no husband and that he came all the way to Marry her," recalled a friend, "and if she was willing he wanted it done right off." Sarah hesitated, telling Thomas that she first needed to pay off "Some little debts" before she could leave Elizabethtown. His eagerness—his desperation, really—was such that he asked for a list of the debts, spent the evening going about the area settling Sarah's accounts, and then married her the following day. They left immediately thereafter for Indiana.[39]

Sarah had apparently at least partly rebuilt her finances following her first husband's death, for she brought with her into the marriage a considerable quantity of household goods and furniture, so much so that Thomas hired help to transport everything to Indiana. She also brought to the Lincoln household her three children, daughters Elizabeth and Matilda and son John.[40]

What she found when she arrived probably left her speechless: a squalid cabin with "no floor or Door to the House of her Husband, no furniture of any Kind, no Beds or Bedding or scarcely any." The inhabitants were, if anything, an even sorrier spectacle, grown "wild—ragged and dirty." She immediately set to work. Sarah "soaped—rubbed and washed the children clean so that they looked pretty neat," Dennis recalled. "She sewed and mended their clothes and the children once more looked human as their own good mother left them."[41]

Thomas seems to have been painfully aware that he was leading his new bride a step or two down the social ladder, so to speak, from a nice little home in a nice little Kentucky town to a rather threadbare cabin in the Indiana woods. Before they left Elizabethtown, he tried to build up the Little Pigeon Creek residence a bit, telling Sarah that he possessed a fine four-post bed with a top. When she arrived she discovered that the bed was a homemade affair constructed of rough-hewn hickory. The "top" was a single pole that he had erected behind the bed but was too tall for the little place, so he had bored a hole in the wall through which it protruded. "She stood in the doorway and looked at it and looked at it," remembered a family member, "and then she laughed."[42]

Sarah was willing to tolerate such primitive surroundings only to a point, and she was not much inclined to subordinate her will to that of her new husband. Harking back to her upbringing in a reasonably prosperous family, and likely also in reaction to the years of penury she had suffered while married to Dennis Johnston, she insisted that Thomas install a wooden floor, a door, and windows in the cabin. When he wanted her to sell some of the furniture she had brought from Elizabethtown, particularly a nice bureau, "saying it was too fine for them to keep," according to Augustus Chapman, "this she refused to do."[43] If Nancy had tried to install the rudiments of an ideal early nineteenth-century domestic household, Sarah was able by force of circumstances and her strong will to take matters at least a little farther.

Everyone who knew her agreed she was a tough, resourceful, and conscientious woman, "of great energy, of remarkable good sense, [and] very industrious," thought Chapman. She was tidy and well mannered, and she immediately took over all the tasks involving food preparation, cleaning, and laundry that had occupied Nancy's time and attention. She handled any trading that was necessary with the neighbors, and she took charge of child-rearing duties.[44]

That last task must have been challenging, presiding as she did over what in modern times is called a "blended family." Chapman later claimed that the three Johnston children and the two Lincoln children were perfectly compatible: "the 2 Setts of Children got along finely together as if they had al[l] have been the children of the same parents," he wrote. As a general rule this was probably true; there is no evidence of serious discord among the children or between them and Sarah. Yet there were surely squabbles and disagreements of various sorts, as well as simply different temperaments. Matilda Johnston later remembered an incident in which her brother, John, delightedly smashed a turtle against a tree, whereupon young Abraham took it upon himself to preach a little impromptu sermon against animal cruelty. Sarah would have had to smooth over these sorts of rough edges, where the Johnston and Lincoln pieces of the family mosaic did not fit together quite so neatly. As a stepmother, her position was surely not easy.[45]

Whether she was able to perform the educational tasks of a good American "republican mother" is difficult to say. Friends and neighbors described her as uneducated, but she did bring with her to Indiana, along with her furniture and fine bureau, several books that Abraham later read. She strongly encouraged him to do so, though it may well have been that she was illiterate.[46]

Sarah and several others later claimed that she grew especially fond of young Abraham. "Abe was a good boy," Sarah later said. "[He] never gave me a cross word or look and never refused in fact, or even in appearance, to do anything I requested [of] him." "She was doubtless the first person that ever treated him like a human being," recalled a friend. Chapman similarly wrote, "She took an esp[ec]ial liking to young Abe, her love for him was warmly returned and continued to the day of his death."[47]

Some of this may well be the hyperbole indulged in by many of Lincoln's friends and relatives after his death. Yet the notion of an affectionate relationship between Lincoln and his stepmother was borne out by Lincoln himself. In his 1860 campaign autobiography, he wrote that Sarah "proved a good and kind mother." It was a terse statement, but coming from a man who only very rarely mentioned his biological mother and sister, and had nothing much good to say about his father, this was high praise indeed.[48]

Thomas Lincoln, Abraham Lincoln's father. Although sometimes rumored to be "shiftless," he was actually a hardworking, if somewhat hapless, Indiana farmer and carpenter. Courtesy of the University Archives, Carnegie-Vincent Library of Lincoln Memorial University, Harrogate, Tennessee.

Sarah Bush Lincoln, Abraham Lincoln's stepmother. After the death of his mother, Nancy, Abraham grew very fond of Sarah, and she of him.

Grave of Nancy Hanks Lincoln. She is buried on a small knoll near the site of the Lincoln farm in Spencer County, Indiana. Author's collection.

Replica of the cabin in which Abraham Lincoln lived during most of his time in Indiana. Author's collection.

FATHER AND SON

A braham was twelve years old in 1821—at the end of childhood, with youth and teenage years still to come. Physically he was outsize, "long and tall," so much so that he routinely grew out of the clothes his new stepmother could sew for him. "His breeches didn't and his socks didn't meet by twelve inches," according to a neighbor, revealing "shinbones sharp, blue and narrow." He was by now big and strong enough to do serious manual labor, "a stout and powerful boy," and in this regard an asset to his father.[1]

Thomas needed the help. Those first three years in Indiana had been hard; scratching a working farm out of the southern Indiana soil was no easy task, and Nancy's untimely death surely cast a pall over the entire family. But by 1821 his new wife had household and child-rearing matters well in hand, and he could concentrate on earning a living. "Mr. Lincoln and Mrs. Lincoln each worked ahead at their own business," Dennis Hanks recalled.[2]

Thomas's "business" was just that: a farm that had to make some money. He purchased the original tract in 1817 on what amounted to a credit system. The land cost him $2 an acre at a total price of $320, but he acquired it by paying only a small percentage, one-twentieth of the amount, when he filed his claim. The rest was due in installments over the next four years.[3]

Those installments were a significant financial burden, because the national economy was weak following a serious economic downturn. The actual causes of the Panic of 1819 took place far over the heads of ordinary farmers like Lincoln, with decisions made by bankers, political leaders, and high-end speculators, but the ripple effect downward to Little Pigeon Creek and other such locales was palpable enough. Thomas would have found the prices he could command when selling his corn and wheat steadily dropping from 1819 well into 1821. This meant less money in his pocket and the distinct possibility that he would be unable to make the next payments on the farm.[4]

Indiana was fortunately one of the few states at the time that prohibited imprisonment for debt, so at least Thomas knew he would not go to jail if his farm failed. The government also passed relief laws allowing farmers more time to pay off their land. In September 1821 Thomas—along with many other struggling farmers nationwide—applied for an extension, playing for time until the economy rebounded and he could get higher prices for his produce.

That extension was no doubt a godsend. But beyond this, the government did little to address the plight of farmers living on the edge of poverty and ruin, and if they went over the edge, their prospects were either charity at the hands of a church or sympathetic relatives or the proverbial "poorhouse," a residential institution normally operated on a shoestring state or county budget and carrying with it an awful social stigma. Soon after becoming a state, Indiana authorized the creation of poorhouses administered by county-level authorities, but only one such place existed in 1821, in Knox County. The state was far more interested in encouraging county officials, the "overseers of the poor," to simply bind impoverished people (often children) out as "apprentices" whenever possible, whereby they became a source of cheap, forced manual labor, with employers merely enjoined to keep the level of work "moderate."[5]

Moderate or not, it was a prospect greeted by someone like Thomas Lincoln with horror. He lived in a time when most people associated poverty with moral failing. A man was poor not because of mere bad luck or something as impersonal as the Panic of 1819; he was poor because he had somehow sinned, because he lacked something in his character—drive, determination, "gumption." No man wanted to fall so far as the poorhouse or apprenticed labor for themselves or their families, in large part because to do so was to abdicate a fundamental part of manhood. If a man could not prosper, he could at least persevere, and he could do so alone, without any handouts—the quintessential "self-made man." While frontier farmers like Thomas often helped each other with various laboring tasks, if they wanted to maintain their self-respect, they absolutely did not seek aid from a government entity or official.[6]

Some avoided the stigma of poor relief by trying to scratch out a daily existence in the thick Hoosier woods. The state knew a fair number of such marginalized and penniless people, "rude, and even abandoned characters," as a British traveler through the state described them, who "retire, with the wolves, from the regular colonists, keeping always to the outside of civilized settlements. They rely for subsistence upon their rifle, and a scanty cultivation of corn, and live in great poverty and privation, a degree only short of the savage state of the Indians."[7]

A few missteps on the farm, a bad judgment call here or there about his crops, or maybe just a run of bad luck—Thomas would have known just how easily he and his family might find themselves at the very bottom of the Indiana barrel. He possessed few resources to fall back on, should times turn really bad. In fact, he now had relatives whose own ill fortune made *him* the fallback plan: Dennis and Sophia, both of whom lived with the Lincolns following the Sparrows' death. Nor was it a small matter that Sarah, for all her welcome assistance, had also brought three children from her first marriage, John, Elizabeth, and Matilda, ranging in age from ten to fourteen.

Thomas did have a lot of help. Abraham, Dennis, and John were fast growing into hardy young men, and they were joined in 1823 by still another Hanks relative, cousin John Hanks, all of whom were well able to wield an ax or push a plow. The younger children could also contribute in various ways. But Thomas certainly had a lot of mouths to feed and bore the weight of serious familial responsibilities. He "now hurried his farming," Dennis later rather cryptically remembered of the time after Sarah and her children arrived at Little Pigeon Creek. Just what he meant by this is unclear, but it does suggest a sense of urgency on Thomas's part to quickly get the farm in good working order so he could provide for his now much larger family.[8]

Besides farming, he had one other primary source of income: carpentry. While growing up in Kentucky, Thomas had learned the trade from his future wife's uncle, Joseph Hanks, who ran a shop in Elizabethtown. He learned "joiner's work," constructing doorsills and window frames, as well as laying floors, installing stairs, and roofing. He was able to build cabinets and simple cabin furniture, and he had built Nancy's coffin, along with the coffins for the other local victims of the "milk sickness." He could also perform more intricate work; a family member later recalled that he constructed the "little wheels" for household spinning machines.[9]

But all this offered only a limited supplement to the farm income. Thomas's skill level may have been partly to blame, as he seems to have been only somewhat competent. Several extant pieces of furniture attributed to him show quality craftsmanship, but one friend called him a "tolerable Country house Carpenter," and another referred to him less charitably as a "Kind of rough Carpenter." While living in Kentucky, Thomas had actually been sued by a customer for shoddy workmanship. But skill level aside, carpentry was simply too unpredictable to constitute a reliable source of income. "He worked at this trade in the winter at odd times," Dennis Hanks remembered. Sometimes Thomas's neighbors might require his carpentry services, sometimes not.[10]

On such shaky ground did Thomas Lincoln plant his feet: farming, with its caprice of market demand, weather, blight, and the like, and a sporadic carpentry practice buoyed only by his uneven abilities and uncertain local demand. His Indiana farm, his "business," was akin to a tiny, fragile ship, tossed about by a stormy sea of forces over which he had little control. His way of riding the ship through the storm was to engage in as many different small business enterprises as possible, hoping that the whole would be greater than the sum of its parts and stay afloat. He sold a little corn here, some hogs and tobacco there, grew what he could to eat, and built a cabinet or installed a door frame when the opportunity arose. He cast about for other ways to make a little money. Sometime soon after arriving at Little Pigeon Creek, he built a horse-powered mill for grinding corn, which only "would make good chicken feed now—but we were glad to get it then," a friend ruefully remembered. Dennis also recalled that Thomas engaged in other "mechanical work," whatever this meant.[11]

Nathaniel Grigsby accurately, if condescendingly, characterized Thomas as "a piddler [who was] always doing but doing nothing great." People liked him; he was an amiable sort, "good humoured [and] sociable and never appeared to be offended." But however pleasant his company, he was to his friends and neighbors a bit of a nonentity: a "plain unpretending plodding man" who simply "attended to his work."[12]

The fact that he was a "plodding man" who moved slowly, was "not nervous," and rarely lost his temper gave an overall impression of contentment. Thomas "most of the time was comfortable and happy," thought Dennis Hanks, "and [he] realized that the sleep of the laboring man was sweet." He was markedly simple in his tastes, "a very Hearty eater but cared Little what kind of food he had," recalled a friend, and he "was satisfied if he had plenty corn Brod [*sic*] and Milk." Here was a man, it might have been argued, who had found happiness in the fact that he needed only a little to get by and was pleased with the pittance he possessed. He "had but few wants and supplied these," believed Grigsby, and "he wanted few things and supplied them easily."[13]

But appearances could be deceiving. He may have been "exceedingly good humored," but Thomas nevertheless led a hard and chancy life, lived under the relentless burden of his obligation to see that little farm succeed, realize some profits from his carpentry work, and generally piece together enough resources to stay solvent. Abraham later described himself as pursuing odd jobs to be able to "procure bread, and keep body and soul together."[14] It was a telling phrase, fully applicable to his father, the difference being that Thomas was obligated to keep "body and soul" together for an entire family. Thomas had to be a provider.

To his credit, he never seems to have tried to shirk this duty nor complained about its many importunities and difficulties. And he was in fact a provider. His family seems to have always had sufficient food to eat, clothes enough to wear (however ill fitting, at least in

Abraham's case), and the other basic necessities of life. The Lincoln farm did not fail, and Thomas was never driven into the poorhouse or the ranks of the "savages" in the woods.[15]

But neither did he ever achieve much in the way of real security. His carpentry was erratic, his mill and other similar operations ramshackle, his farm produce meager enough to produce little in the way of a surplus. "It is generally supposed that Thomas Lincoln was a farmer," recalled George Balch, a neighbor from Thomas's later Illinois days, "and such he was, if one who tilled so little land by such primitive modes could be so called." While other farmers hauled their produce for sale in wagons, Thomas could fit his in a basket or even a large tray. "Sometimes he stowed a large portion of them under his bed," Balch said.[16]

Balch's memories dated from Thomas's later years in Illinois, when his failing health and circumstances rendered his situation more difficult than during his Indiana days. Still, Thomas and his family lived one step ahead of ruin even in Little Pigeon Creek, a perpetual life of just enough. "It was pretty pinching times," Abraham later remarked about those first years in Indiana. They "presently got reasonably comfortable" after Sarah arrived, as he put it, but such was all Thomas was ever really able to achieve—keeping the family reasonably comfortable.[17]

Some chalked this up to a lack of basic management skills. He was "V[er]y careless about his business," recalled Augustus Chapman, and "a poor Manager [who] at time[s] accumulated considerable property which he always managed to make way with about as fast as he made it." Thomas's bookkeeping, such as it was, bordered on the laughable. One person who visited Thomas as an old man while living in Illinois remembered him tracking some millwork he performed for neighboring farmers by using charcoal marks on the wall of his cabin. Thomas "had taken a fire-coal and drawn four black marks on the face of a joist, something like the four bars of music," he recalled, "and when he sold a customer a peck of meal he simply reached up and drew his fingers through the lower line; for two pecks, he rubbed a hole through two of the lines," and so forth. "'The simplest thing in the world,' said he."[18]

Thomas was also hampered by his lack of education and general illiteracy. Abraham later stated that his father "never did more in the way of writing than to bunglingly sign his own name." Others suggested a somewhat higher level of skill, though not by much. A neighbor remembered Thomas reading the Bible and being able to write a bit, though added that he was "not a good reader or scholar." Cousin John Hanks did not think Thomas could write at all, but he "could read [a] little."[19]

This left him vulnerable to mistakes, misunderstandings, and worse. One Indiana neighbor told of Thomas's business dealings with a fellow farmer named Carter, who had worked out a deal to purchase a small portion of Thomas's land. Knowing of Thomas's inability to read, Carter placed a document before him that would have actually meant the sale of the entire Lincoln farm. Fortunately, Thomas thought to give the paper to Abraham, who scanned it and promptly told his father he was about to be cheated. "If you sign that deed, you have sold the farm," Abraham declared.[20]

Perhaps Thomas's lack of a father played a role in his evident inability to focus and concentrate his energies persistently enough and long enough to acquire a decent education, properly manage his finances, or much of anything else. In an age dominated by agricultural work, fathers usually toiled alongside their sons in the fields and were expected to impart lessons of self-discipline, perseverance, focus, and application to and completion of tasks. After their father was felled by that Shawnee bullet in the western Virginia woods, Thomas and his brothers were scattered, each to pursue his own ends. Thomas was apparently left more or less on his own, caring for his aging mother in Elizabethtown and doing what he could to get by without much in the way of either an education or the fatherly guidance that often took the place of a schoolhouse. He subsequently became Grigsby's "piddler," having learned that the only answer for him was to elevate quantity over quality, placing many irons in the fire—farming, carpentry, millwork—at once but never giving any one thing the amount of attention necessary to thrive.[21]

Thomas did find solace in some quiet pastimes that relieved the dreariness and monotony of daily rural life. He greatly enjoyed hunting. His family depended to at least some extent on the wild game he could bring to the table from the surrounding woods, but he "delighted in having a good hunt," beyond whatever the necessities of life and putting food on the table required. Augustus Chapman remembered that Thomas "always Kept a fine Rifle," though curiously he did not have an equal passion for fishing.[22]

Wrestling was a prime sporting and social pursuit in early rural America, and Thomas was a good wrestler. It was a pursuit to which he was physically well suited, with his low, stocky build. "He was a large man of great muscular power," Dennis Hanks claimed, and "was built so compact that it was difficult to find or feel a rib in his body." Several acquaintances remembered that while living in Kentucky, Thomas and a man named Hardin engaged in a "long and tedious fight" in front of a large crowd of their neighbors, from which Thomas emerged the victor.[23]

He was something of an extroverted sort, "a social man [who] loved company," with "Back[w]oodsish" but easygoing manners that made for good conversation. He was "passionately fond of humerous [sic] jokes and stories," wrote neighbor William Greene. It was a predilection he passed on to his son, though according to Dennis, "Thomas Lincoln the father of Abraham could beat his son telling a story [or] cracking a joke."[24]

Thomas also found comfort in his faith. He was a regular church-going man, attending first in Kentucky and then in Indiana Baptist churches with a strong Calvinistic bent, emphasizing a literal interpretation of the Bible and God's saving grace from the womb until death. The Little Pigeon Creek church was a Separatist Baptist congregation—a bit less gloomy and fatalistic than their more conservative Hardshell Baptist brothers and sisters, perhaps, but nevertheless serious Calvinist Christians. On any given Sunday Thomas and his family would have heard strictures against sinful living in all its forms, and Thomas took the ministers at their word. He rarely drank—indulging only in an occasional hot toddy at Christmas—or gambled, and he was "not profane." "He was a good quiet citizen, [of] moral habits," John Hanks remembered.[25]

Some saw in Thomas a severely limited, perhaps even dull-witted, man of only marginal competence. One person who knew him sneered that Thomas was nothing more than "an excellent species of poor white trash"; another called him a "perfect greenhorn." Later generations of Americans often picked up on this theme, the better to romanticize Abraham Lincoln's remarkable rise to glory, given his father's dubious character: Thomas "was as lazy as loafing, as shiftless as could be, and as poor as poverty," read a late nineteenth-century biography of Lincoln, in a chapter titled "How Something Came from Nothing." If George Washington's father of myth was the paragon of virtue who would not punish his wayward son for chopping down the cherry tree, Abraham Lincoln's father was such a sorry lout that only a miracle of divine intervention could explain his son's later greatness.[26]

But those who took Thomas Lincoln for a ne'er-do-well misunderstood him and his situation. He established a functioning farm from almost nothing in the unforgiving Indiana woods, he weathered the death of his first wife and successfully remarried, he assumed without apparent complaint the burden of caring for not just his own children but also others who were more distant relatives, and he did so while avoiding the more common vices of his day. A "piddler" he may have been, but he was never a pauper, still less a "savage." He lived out his days somewhere between success and failure, and if he might have done better with more drive and ambition, he also might have done much worse.

Abraham understood that his father had been dealt a hard hand. When as an adult he wrote two brief political autobiographies, he made it a point to emphasize that Thomas had lost his own father at an early age and was forced to grow up in very straitened circumstances, "litterally [sic] without education" and "even in childhood a wandering laboring boy." But however much Abraham appreciated his father's difficulties, and however much Thomas would later feel a degree of happiness for Abraham and his accomplishments—"Mr. Lincoln was proud of Abraham while in Congress," remembered a neighbor—father and son were far from close.[27]

At exactly what point their relationship became troubled is difficult to pinpoint. Some believed a degree of alienation was always present between them. Thomas "never showed by his actions that he thought much of his son Abraham when a Boy," believed Augustus Chapman. "He treated him rather unkind than otherwise." Chapman thought that Thomas was much fonder of his stepson, John, who, like Thomas, was a not overly ambitious farmboy of limited ambition and talent.[28]

Others thought that young Abraham was too much of a smart aleck for his father's tastes and lacked a sense of propriety around adults. "Abe was one of those forward boys," recalled Dennis Hanks, describing him as a gregarious sort who "always would have the first word." When passersby sometimes stopped at the Lincoln farm for information, Abraham would perch on a nearby fence and begin jabbering away, to the point that Thomas felt compelled to "Nock [*sic*] him down of[f] the fence." Abraham's reaction, Dennis remembered, was to drop "a kind of silent unwelcome tear, as evidence of his sensations—or other feelings."[29]

Abraham also liked to mimic local preachers and politicians, clambering atop a stump or fence to deliver a humorous and apparently spot-on lampoon, which struck his father as both disrespectful and a frivolous waste of time. According to Sarah, her husband would grow incensed as Abraham "quit his own work to speak and made the other children as well as the men quit their work." "This practice of 'preaching' and political speaking, into which Abe had fallen, at length became a great nuisance to old Tom," wrote Abraham's friend and fellow lawyer Ward Hill Lamon, who "was compelled to break it up with a strong hand; and poor Abe was many times dragged from the platform, and hustled off to his work in no gentle manner."[30]

Thomas disciplined his son with physical punishment. This was not at all an unusual practice among fathers and sons in those days, but it occurred frequently enough that people noticed. Thomas "would not whip Abe or scold him before folk," said one observer, "but he would take him by himself and tend to him after they was gone. People in them days believed that whipping was good for children."[31]

Abraham's inveterate reading habits also caused friction. "Abe was not energetic except in one thing—he was active and persistent in learning," recalled his stepsister Matilda. Thomas was not entirely averse to this. He allowed Abraham to take advantage of what little schooling was sporadically available in the Little Pigeon Creek area, and Sarah Lincoln denied that her husband tried to actively discourage Abraham from reading while at home. "As a usual thing Mr. Lincoln never made Abe quit reading to do anything if he could avoid it," she claimed. "He would do it himself first." While this may be a case of Sarah trying to protect the memory of her husband from accusations of a callous disregard for his son's ambitions, others who lived in the Little Pigeon Creek area agreed. "When Abe was reading his father Made it a rule never to ask [*sic*] him to lay down a book," thought neighbor Joseph Richardson.[32]

But while Thomas may not have tried to actively hinder Abraham's studies, his son's dedication to reading was a source of annoyance and frustration. Thomas "had a[n] old Grey horse and he was not able to plow as much as abe was," recalled a neighbor, "and abe while the horse Rested had his paper pen and ink out in the field." Later Americans would see in such habits an admirable dedication to learning in one who became a future president, but at the time this seemed to his father a lack of attentiveness to the things that really mattered on a farm—and the things that really mattered to Thomas the provider. "His father being a day labourer [*sic*] and without education—looked upon bone and mussel sufficient to make a man," mused a friend, "and, that time spent in school as doubly wasted." Abraham later implied that he was able to undertake serious study of subjects like English and math only after he "had separated from his father."[33]

Here, perhaps, is where the relentless pressures of maintaining the farm and feeding the family manifested, where Thomas could ill afford to be so good-humored and amiable in the treatment of a son who seemed preoccupied with reading at the expense of the sort of labor Thomas badly needed him to perform. To modern Americans, he can seem a heartless and unkind father who tried to callously deprive a future president of his destiny by denying him an education in the name of putting in a corn crop or performing some other menial task. But for Thomas the wolves were nearly always at the door, waiting in the guise of that Knox County poorhouse, or worse, to devour his family. If he demanded that Abraham put down the books and grab a plow handle, he had better reasons for doing so than future generations of Abraham Lincoln's admirers would often care to admit.

More generally, father and son simply shared little in common, aside from their love of wrestling and jokes. Abraham detested the hunting trips that Thomas enjoyed; he later wrote with a degree of satisfaction that after he shot that wild turkey during those early days in Indiana, he had "never since pulled a trigger on larger game." He was also not nearly as inclined toward religion as his father. "Abe had no particular religion," his stepmother believed, and "didn't think of that question at that time [growing up in Indiana], if he ever did." To a man like Thomas, who took churchgoing seriously, this must have rankled.[34]

So did Abraham's general attitude toward the various occupations that constituted Thomas's everyday life. While Abraham seems to have sometimes helped Thomas in his carpentry, there is no evidence that he particularly enjoyed that sort of work, and he absolutely did not like plowing and harvesting in the fields. One day while working as a hired laborer in a cornfield owned by the Crawford family, he remarked, "Mrs. Crawford, I don't always intend to delve, grub, shuck corn, split rails and the like." People remembered his diligence in reading and studying, more so than grubbing and shucking, and his motivation at least in part was to use the former to escape the latter. "He didn't like physical labor," Sarah Lincoln recalled, and his father's life was all about physical labor.[35]

Even other hard jobs were a welcome respite, as long as he broke free of the fields. "The dull routine of chores and household errands in the boy's everyday life was brightened now and then by a visit to the mill," Herndon later wrote. "I often in later years heard Mr. Lincoln say that going to the mill gave him the greatest pleasure of his boyhood days." The trip was seven miles, and running the hand-operated mill was difficult work, but at least it got him off the farm for a while and away from his father.[36]

"Lincoln said to me one day that his father taught him to work but never learned him to love it," remembered a neighboring farmer. Worst of all, when Abraham did manage to earn a bit of money by doing odd jobs in the area, Thomas demanded his son's wages—every cent. He was well within his rights as a father; the law recognized his power to keep any money his children might acquire. But it struck young Abraham as a singular injustice to turn over to Thomas the fruits of his labor. Years later he would grimly refer to this arrangement as a form of "slavery" that he was forced to endure.[37]

By the time Abraham was in his early teens, he exhibited at the very least a certain coolness toward Thomas. "I Never Could tell whether Abe Loved his farther [*sic*] Very well or Not," Dennis Hanks later admitted.[38] The simmering hostility between father and son manifested in a variety of minor but telling ways. As a prank Abraham and his stepbrother John once tried to sew a coonskin around Thomas's favorite dog, an "insignificant little cur" that ran in a blind panic toward home and was then killed by several larger dogs. "Father was much incensed," Abraham later noted. Such little incidents, along with the two males' different temperaments, Thomas's evident need to squeeze from Abraham as much labor as possible, and Abraham's ambition to accomplish more than his father ever had and to make something of himself—all added up to a strained and emotionally distant relationship by the time Abraham entered his teenage years.[39]

As an adult, Abraham seemed determined to have as little as possible to do with his father, whom he increasingly looked at as a source of embarrassment. "I very cheerfully send you the twenty dollars, which sum you say is necessary to save your land from sale," Abraham wrote to his father in 1848 by way of his stepbrother, John, who could read what Thomas could not. He then added, "It is singular that you should have forgotten a judgment against you; and it is more singular that the plaintiff should have let you forget it so long, particularly as I suppose you have always had property enough to satisfy a judgment of that amount. Before you pay it, it would be well to be sure you have not paid it."

In a longer accompanying letter to John, Abraham was considerably lacking in cheerfulness, and he let John (and by extension Thomas) know exactly how he felt. "You are not *lazy*, and still you *are* an *idler*," Abraham wrote. "I doubt whether since I saw you, you have done a good whole day's work in any one day. You do not very much dislike to work; and still you do not work much, merely because it does not seem to you that you could get much for it. This habit of uselessly wasting time, is the whole difficulty; and it is vastly important to you, and still more so to your children that you should break this habit. It is more important to them, because they have longer to live, and can keep out of an idle habit before they are in it; easier than they can get out after they are in."[40]

Calling John an "idler" was not far from Grigsby's description of Thomas as a "piddler," and while Abraham was particularly annoyed in 1848 because of John's and his father's regular habits of both bungling their affairs and begging Abraham for money, it is not difficult to see strong echoes here of something deeper—of a lifelong rejection of his father's entire way of life, his lack of ambition and his inability to provide for himself and his family little more than a hand-to-mouth existence. That little bit of parenting advice Abraham gave to his stepbrother was telling as well; by 1848 Abraham had become a fairly successful middle-class lawyer, having escaped his father's "idle habit," and he apparently felt justified in admonishing his stepbrother to at least try to help his own children do the same by setting a better example than had his own father.

The relationship between Thomas and Abraham remained chilly until the end. When in 1851 Abraham was informed that Thomas lay mortally ill and wished to find some way to reconcile with his son, his response was unenthusiastic. "Say to him that if we could meet now, it is doubtful whether it would not be more painful than pleasant," he wrote to John.[41] He did not visit his father's deathbed, nor did he attend the funeral.

GROWING

Change was in the air at the Lincoln farm when Abraham celebrated his sixteenth birthday in 1825.

His sister, Sarah, left the Little Pigeon Creek home that year to live with the Crawford family, exchanging her room and board for housework. She made a positive impression on the Crawfords and others around her. "She was a good, kind amiable girl," Elizabeth Crawford thought, and had inherited her mother's intelligence and general sociability. "Her good humored laugh I can see now," recalled Nathaniel Grigsby. "She could like her brother Abe meet and greet a person with the very kindest greeting in the world."[1]

Nathaniel's older brother, Aaron, found Sarah particularly winsome, and they married in August 1826. They settled in a cabin a few miles away, and Aaron took up farming, like his family and most of his neighbors. He seems to have been an industrious man, eventually accumulating nearly $300 worth of property and livestock.[2] But his marriage came to a tragic end less than two years later, when Sarah died while giving birth to a stillborn child. A story later arose that Aaron refused to send for a doctor to treat his distressed wife until it was too late. Whether this was true or not, Abraham reacted as any bereaved brother might: he "sat down on a log and hid his face in his hands while the tears rolled down." Both Sarah and her child were buried in the cemetery of the Little Pigeon Creek Baptist Church. Abraham rarely spoke of his sister again, only briefly noting in one of his campaign autobiographies that she had "died many years ago, leaving no child."[3]

Dennis Hanks had also left the Lincoln home by 1825. Four years earlier he had married Sarah Elizabeth Johnston, Abraham's fifteen-year-old stepsister. Theirs must have been a whirlwind courtship, for they married less than a year after Elizabeth's arrival in Indiana. They raised a family of their own, having four children, but remained close to the Lincolns and later accompanied Thomas and his wife and children when they relocated to Illinois. "I was an actor pretty much all my life in the scene" of the Lincolns' lives, Dennis later boasted. This was a considerable exaggeration; still, he had been a steady fixture in Abraham's everyday life since they had all landed at Thompson's Ferry nine years previously. His sudden absence from the pallets they both shared in the loft of the Lincoln cabin must have seemed odd to Abraham.[4]

Sophia Hanks probably left the Lincoln farm as well at about this time, though exactly when and under what circumstances is unknown. She had lived with the Lincolns since the milk sickness killed the Sparrow couple, and she seems to have stayed for several years. Eventually she married and settled in the Ozark region of Arkansas, where she bore three children. Sophia fell out of touch with her Lincoln and Hanks relatives, so much so that during the war she wrote Dennis to ask him whether the president of the United States was in fact her cousin. "Is this not Strange to you it was to me," a bemused Dennis subsequently wrote to Lincoln.[5]

Sophia later told her children that she recalled accompanying Abraham to one of the local "blab schools" in the area—so called because of the prevalence of rote recitation as a method of learning. "She remembered that it was a long walk, about three and a half miles," said her son. Abraham would begin practicing his "blabbing" long before they arrived, shouting out his lessons as they walked, "so that he was audible at a considerable distance from the path."[6]

When Abraham and his cousin finally reached their destination, they entered a time-honored early American institution: the little one-room schoolhouse, wherein farmers' children sat on long benches or behind small wooden desks and worked to better themselves and perhaps rise to a higher station in life than their parents. This was the foundation of the American Dream, the notion that hard work at an early age to master basic knowledge and literacy was the key to success. As an adult, Lincoln extolled education's supreme virtue in a democracy, declaring in an early political speech, "I view it as the most important subject which we as a people can be engaged in. . . . That every man may receive at least, a moderate education, and thereby be enabled to read the histories of his own and other countries, by which he may duly appreciate the value of our free institutions, appears to be an object of vital importance."[7]

Few would have disputed this sentiment. Yet the truth, especially in a remote rural area like Little Pigeon Creek, was more complicated. Indiana possessed nothing that could be construed as a public education system in the early nineteenth century; but then neither did most other American states. The various reforms and practices associated with modern education—professionally trained teachers, separation of students into different grades based on age, commonly accepted teaching strategies such as using older pupils to help their struggling younger peers—were still some years in the future.

In terms of overall education policy, Indiana was actually a bit more progressive than most states. Formed under the auspices of the 1787 Northwest Ordinance, with its provision that a portion of land sales from each township be set aside to fund public education, Indiana in its first constitution indicated that the new state would "provide by law for a general system of education . . . wherein tuition shall be gratis, and open to all." Acting on this language, the state did provide funds to establish Indiana's first institution of higher education, in Vincennes (what would eventually become Vincennes University), and the first governor, Jonathan Jennings, urged the state assembly to act quickly on its constitutional provisions and begin creating a comprehensive system for "the dissemination of useful knowledge[, which] will be indispensably necessary as a support to morals and a restraint to vice."[8]

But words did not translate into much action. Land had been set aside to be leased for school construction as far back as 1808, and "Trustees of School Lands" were appointed in each Indiana township, tasked with overseeing the schools' construction and operation. But these trustees were given very little actual money, and aside from the larger and more progressive towns like Vincennes and Evansville, few communities possessed viable public schools by 1820.[9]

Hoosiers who wanted their children to receive an education instead relied on their own resources. They provided the school building, often a little log box not much larger than Thomas Lincoln's Little Pigeon Creek cabin. One typical schoolhouse of the time was described as follows: "Upon entering the door, we had to step down the breadth of one log to reach the floor. . . . The fire was built on the ground. About three feet from the floor, holes were left between the logs for windows, the light being admitted through panes of greased paper."[10]

In addition to construction of the building, parents usually defrayed the costs of the building's maintenance, firewood for heat in the winter, and whatever rudimentary supplies they could scrounge. Furniture was often minimal; one account of an Indiana schoolhouse said it "had seats of puncheon, and desks it knew not."[11] Most of all, tuition was required to pay the schoolmaster. These men (they were nearly always male) were usually not professionally trained teachers, and even though Indiana in 1824 tried to institute a rudimentary licensing system, schoolmasters varied widely in their level of education, experience, and educational methods. Those methods were confined to rote memorization and recitation ("blab"), interspersed with a liberal application of corporal punishment, "beating their pupils like oxen," as one observer ruefully put it. Sometimes they knew a great deal about their subjects, but on other occasions not so much. "No qualification was ever required of a teacher," Lincoln later laconically observed, and "if a straggler supposed to understand latin, happened to so-journ in the neighborhood, he was looked upon as a wizzard [sic]."[12]

In their defense, schoolmasters did not have an easy job. Their patience was often tried to the limit by unruly pupils, whose attendance could be quite erratic—determined by the vicissitudes of seasonal farm chores—and whose motivation was uneven at best. Nor was the money much of an incentive; their salaries were so meager that schoolmasters usually could not even afford a home of their own but were instead compelled to board with a nearby family.[13]

Such was Indiana's slapdash school "system." Most Hoosiers were probably much like Thomas Lincoln: well intentioned regarding their children's education but tending to have higher priorities, such as getting in the crops, feeding their families, paying off their farms, and avoiding the various calamities that were ever present in Indiana's harsh environment. "The great need of the people for liberal training was obscured by more immediate wants and pressing dangers," wrote an early historian of Indiana. Plows and axes took precedence over books.[14]

Lincoln's experiences were well within this norm. He and his sister briefly attended two schools in Kentucky run by Zachariah Riney and Caleb Hazel, two respectable but limited schoolmasters. Both Abraham and Sarah were so young at this point that they likely learned little beyond the basics of letters and numbers; Lincoln later called these "A.B.C." schools.[15] In Indiana Abraham attended local schools "by littles," as he put it, run by Andrew Crawford, James Swaney, and Azel Dorsey, three men all pretty much indistinguishable from each other or from his Kentucky instructors. The schoolhouse was located near a spring on the outskirts of Gentryville, a "kind of hewed log house [with] two chimneys—one door [and] holes for windows." Apparently the use of "greased paper" was a common thing; in the Little Pigeon Creek area schoolhouse, it was "pasted over the holes in winter time to admit light." A nearby oak tree was blackened and burned by the billows of smoke emitted from the twin chimneys.[16]

Loudly reciting his lessons as he walked down the path alongside cousin Sophia, squeezing a few weeks' worth of schooling between harvest times and other chores, hauling threadbare copies of Thomas Dilworth's *New Guide to the English Tongue* (popularly called "Dilworth's Speller"), steadily chalking and erasing math and writing lessons on the back of a wooden shovel by firelight in the cabin on a cold winter evening—these are familiar images of the young Lincoln in American folklore.[17] And these images are for the most part accurate. Friends and relatives who remembered little else about Lincoln's Indiana days, or who contradicted each other in their memories, were unanimous and emphatic on this point:

Abraham was absolutely (some might have said obsessively) committed to "book learning." It was his defining characteristic: "He was always reading, scribbling, writing, ciphering"; he "read diligently . . . got up early and then read"; he "read constantly when he had an opportunity"; "what Lincoln read he read and re-read [and] read and studied thoroughly." He also wrote an occasional poem and practiced math problems: "When he . . . was not going to school he worked out his sums and problems at various times and places." One family story had Lincoln walking twelve miles to obtain a book on grammar after one of his teachers told him he needed to learn the basic structure of the English language.[18]

"The agregate [*sic*] of all [my] schooling did not amount to one year," he later noted, and yet he persevered. It is hard to overstate how keenly and painfully the adult Abraham Lincoln felt this lack of a formal education. In all three of the brief autobiographies he penned, he made his "defective" education a key narrative point. "There was absolutely nothing to excite ambition for education," he wrote, so "of course when I came of age I did not know much. Still somehow, I could read, write, and cipher to the Rule of Three; but that was all."[19]

He tried to compensate for his lack of schoolhouse time with self-education, which was also a challenge. His choice of material was limited by circumstances; there just were not all that many books available. Still, for a boy growing up in such a remote area, he managed to assemble an impressive bibliography for himself.

Most Hoosiers possessed a Bible and a copy of Paul Bunyan's *Pilgrim's Progress*, staples of any good Christian household. Lincoln read both; in all likelihood these were the only books Thomas Lincoln possessed—if he possessed any at all—at least prior to his second marriage.[20] But Abraham was fortunate that his stepmother brought with her several books when she arrived in Indiana, among them Daniel Defoe's *Robinson Crusoe*, which became one of Lincoln's favorites. He also managed to read *Aesop's Fables* and collections of famous speeches such as *The Columbian Orator* (famous for its seminal influence on the young Frederick Douglass) and *The Kentucky*

Preceptor. Other families in the area had assembled little libraries, and Lincoln took full advantage. "When he worked for us he read all our books," Elizabeth Crawford recalled; he "would sit up late in the night, kindle up the fire and read by it."[21]

His method of absorbing what he read involved constant repetition, drilling facts, words, and book passages into his head over and over again by writing them down in a "kind of scrap book." The few sheets that survive from this time, written in a remarkably clear hand, are crowded with numbers, math problems and rules ("when several numbers of Divers Denomination[s] are given to be divided by common division this is called Compound Division"), and even a bit of verse:

> Abraham Lincoln
> His hand and pen
> He will be good but
> god knows When.[22]

If no paper was available, he used boards, writing with charcoal lumps until the board turned black, then cleaning it off and starting over. The point was not the recording of information; rather, the act of copying, after enough applications, embedded an idea firmly in his mind. "He must understand everything, even to the smallest thing, minutely and exactly," his stepmother recalled, "and when it was fixed in his mind to suit him he became easy and he never lost that fact or his understanding of it." It would become a lifelong habit, this slow but steady and deep digestion of mental food, the hallmark of a man who knew how his own mind worked and acted accordingly. "I am slow to learn and slow to forget what I have learned," he later remarked. "My mind is like a piece of steel, very hard to scratch anything on it and almost impossible after you get it there to rub it out."[23]

Lincoln's inveterate reading habits caused difficulties with not only his father but also many of their friends and neighbors, and he acquired a reputation for sloth. According to one local farmer, "Abe was awful lazy: he worked for me [and] was always reading and thinking [and I] used to get mad at him." Books interfered with his social life as well; his stepmother remembered that while her son, John, "was away at dances Abraham was at home with [his] head at [the] fireplace reading or studying."[24]

Sometime in 1825 Lincoln borrowed a biography of George Washington from Elizabeth Crawford's husband, Josiah. Carrying it back to the Lincoln cabin, he put it on a makeshift shelf ("two pins in the wall and a clapboard on them"), where an overnight rainstorm soaked the book. Crawford—a rather dyspeptic sort—did not let Abraham off lightly, making the boy spend several days "pulling blades" in his cornfield (removing the dead leaves of old cornstalks by way of clearing the ground) as repayment. Lincoln felt Crawford's toll for the spoiled Washington biography was unfair and that Crawford "had treated him unkindly in regard to this Book." He got a measure of revenge by composing some rather cutting verses (since lost) regarding Crawford's looks, in particular his very large nose (his nickname in the neighborhood was "Nosey" Crawford). The man seems to have taken it in stride; Dennis Hanks recalled that Lincoln's poetry "made all the neighbors, Crawford included burst their sides with laughter."[25]

Not long after the incident with Crawford's book, Abraham was embroiled in a more serious fray when he used his penchant for poetry to skewer several members of the Grigsby family. He had apparently nursed a smoldering resentment toward Aaron Grigsby ever since Sarah's death. One friend rather cryptically averred to Lincoln's anger regarding Aaron's "cruel treatment of his wife"; it is unclear whether this referred to Aaron's tardiness in summoning a doctor to tend Sarah's labor or some form of abuse.[26]

Whatever the reason, relations were cool between the Lincolns and Grigsbys thereafter. When the Grigsbys failed to invite the Lincolns to a double family wedding for brothers Reuben and Charles, Abraham felt provoked enough to write a satire known locally as the "Chronicles of Reuben." His verse was a parody of the Bible's book of Chronicles and described the two men inadvertently sleeping with the wrong brides. It even cast some aspersions on yet another Grigsby brother, William:

"For Reuben and Charley have married two girls,
But Billy has married a boy. . . .

So Billy and Natty agreed very well
And mamma's well pleased with the match.
The egg is laid, but Natty's afraid
The shell is so soft it never will hatch."[27]

Unlike Crawford, Billy was not at all amused.[28] He angrily challenged Lincoln to a fight. The affair was set to take place at a chosen spot about half a mile from Gentryville. People came from all around to witness the brawl. When the two would-be combatants arrived, Abraham—who was at that point a strapping teenager, big and strong and well over six feet tall—stood aside for his stepbrother, John. John got the worst of it and was "badly hurt," according to eyewitnesses. One later claimed that when his stepbrother began to falter, and when Grigsby stepped outside the fighting ring, thus violating the rules, such as they were, Abraham supposedly "waived a bottle of whiskey over his head" and "swore he was the big buck of the lick," after which ensued a general melee.[29]

Whether this story is true or not (other accounts have the combatants separating more or less peacefully), it does illustrate a not particularly appealing side of Lincoln: the quarreler and composer of verses aimed at belittling people he did not like.[30] At least some of his neighbors thought him rather unkind this way. Augustus Chapman believed the doggerel he composed about "Nosey" Crawford had been written in a "Most unmerciful Manner." One wonders whether at least some of Lincoln's motivation in this regard was using his "book learning" as a weapon in retaliation against so many of his neighbors who thought it was evidence of his laziness.[31]

In any event, his lampooning of "Nosey" Crawford and the "Chronicles of Reuben" affair, along with the subsequent brawl, show Abraham as a rather typical American adolescent boy in that he could sometimes let his emotions get the better of him. He could, like any young man, exercise poor judgment and exhibit a callous disregard for propriety and the feelings of others. Also like any other boy his age, he was not always in complete control of his emotions and sometimes behaved rashly.[32]

He could get into roughhousing fights with friends, and more generally he was fully capable of engaging in the strenuous physical activities common on the Indiana frontier. "He was fond of Exercise such as Jumping Rasling [*sic*] Playing ball and all kinds of fun," remembered a friend. Wrestling was his particular joy; an Illinois friend later claimed that Abraham "loved the sport as well as any man could," and this no doubt extended back into his Indiana days, especially given the advantages his height and build afforded him in a match.[33]

He also had his share of injuries and mishaps such as were common to any boy's life, cuts, scrapes, and bruises so unremarkable that no one then or since much noticed. When he was ten years old, Abraham did experience an injury more serious than most. While accompanying his father to a local mill, he was leveled by a powerful kick from a horse, an experience that left him unconscious. He was "apparently killed for [a?] time," as he later half jokingly put it. He eventually regained consciousness and suffered no lasting damage aside from a lifelong problem with his left eye, which occasionally "floated" slightly out of alignment.[34]

The horse kick was a close call, but it was not a particularly unusual accident for anyone living on the Indiana frontier; and on the whole, much of Abraham's Indiana life seems to have pretty much mirrored the experiences of other young boys coming of age on farms in the early American wilderness. But there were differences too. If he was typical in some respects, he was unusual in others.

Probably his most noticeable uncommon trait—aside from his bookishness—was his physical appearance. As a child he had been thought "gawky," but by the time he entered his teens he was described as "bony and raw," "long and tall," "dangling," "slouchy," or just plain "odd." He was all knees and legs and elbows, his arms seemingly too long for his body—which was saying a lot, given how tall he had become. His angular head was perched atop a thin neck. He towered over his companions; Nathaniel Grigsby estimated that at seventeen or eighteen years of age, Abraham was six feet two inches tall and weighed about 160 pounds, "stout [and] withy-wiry." People struggled to find appropriately picturesque ways of describing him: a "long, thin, gawky boy, dried up and shriveled," was how one woman remembered him.[35]

Clothing was a problem, especially as he continued to grow ever longer and taller. Like most other boys, he wore buckskin along with "linsey woolsey" shirts and coats made from linen that Sarah likely produced on her spinning wheel from flax grown in the farm's fields. When he outgrew these, it was difficult and time-consuming for her to replace them. He was no slob—Sarah described him as "tolerably neat and clean"—but neither did he give too much thought to how he might look, walking around in clothes that were chronically small. Grigsby declared that normally "between the shoe and sock and his britches . . . there was bare and naked six or more inches of Abe Lincoln shinbone"; others thought it was closer to twelve inches.[36]

His appearance likely contributed to his unease around girls. "He didn't go to see the girls much," noted one friend, and Dennis likewise mentioned that he "didn't love the company of girls." One young woman named Anna Gentry, who attended Crawford's school with Abraham when they were both about fifteen years old, thought his aversion to female company stemmed from his association of girls with frivolity—he would rather read a book than socialize in mixed company. Another neighbor believed he was just more comfortable "with the Boys," who he thought could better appreciate his stories and jokes, whereas around girls he "was rather backward."[37]

He was uncommonly tenderhearted, especially toward animals (undoubtedly a factor in his disdain for hunting), and displayed an aversion to boisterous behavior of any kind—enough that he stood out in what was often a quite violent Indiana environment. Nathaniel Grigsby remembered Abraham growing incensed with his playmates when they tortured turtles by setting small fires on their backs; he would "chide us [and] tell us it was wrong." He also had a neighborhood reputation as a peacemaker who stopped more fights than he started. Lincoln may have enjoyed wrestling as a friendly, if occasionally rough, pastime, but if "there was any fiting [sic] about to Commence he would try to stop [it]."[38]

He also had a reputation for extraordinary personal honesty, though assertions to this effect by his friends and family need to be taken with a larger than usual grain of salt, given how strongly the sobriquet "Honest Abe" had attached to him by the time they recorded their reminiscences. Their high praise of the young Abraham Lincoln's integrity has more than a whiff of hyperbole: "He never told me a lie in his life, never equivocated [and] never dodged"; he was a "good, friendly, sociable, honest boy"; he "could not reason falsely [and] if he attempted it he failed." Nathaniel Grigsby gushed that Lincoln was "kind, jocular, witty, wise, honest, just [and] full of human integrity." But exaggeration aside, Lincoln does seem to have been a fundamentally honest and straightforward young man, as multiple Indiana neighbors attested.[39]

He was generally free of profanity and did not use tobacco, two ubiquitous features of frontier life. He was also at best only an occasional consumer of alcohol. As an adult he was a teetotaler, claiming that alcohol made him feel "flabby and undone," but growing up in Indiana, he would have found this practically impossible. Nearly everyone drank some form of alcohol, believing it to be a means of warding off sickness and safer than drinking water. Abraham was no different: "He did drink his dram as well as all others did, preachers and Christians included," said Grigsby.[40]

But sometime in his late teens, his light drinking habits disappeared altogether. A neighbor named William Wood, who had a predilection for politics and current events and often loaned Lincoln copies of the many newspapers to which he subscribed, recalled frequent discussions with the young man on the subject of temperance. Wood subscribed to a temperance newspaper and recalled that "Abe used to borrow it, take it home and read it." Lincoln even tried his hand at writing a temperance article, which Wood later sent to a Baptist minister friend, who had it published in an Ohio temperance paper.[41]

It was a rare moment for the young Lincoln, this serious engagement with such a heavily faith-based idea. Although he was the son of a churchgoing father, mother, and stepmother, and it was an age of serious national religious fervor, the people around Lincoln in

Indiana noticed that he was not especially fervent in his religious beliefs. "I Cant tell But I Dont Think he held any [religious] Views Very Strong," Dennis Hanks later wrote. This is not to say that the young Lincoln was an agnostic or exhibited the traits of serious religious skepticism that later became so prominent and actually laid him open to charges of religious infidelity in his political career. But he was not heavily invested, emotionally or intellectually, in matters of faith. He knew his Bible, and he mixed comfortably with the Baptists of his father's faith and others of a serious Christian bent who surrounded him in Indiana—but not much more. "You wished me to tell you whether Abraham lincoln ever made Any pretensions of religion during his Stay in this country [Indiana]," Elizabeth Crawford wrote to Lincoln's former law partner, William Herndon, after the war. "I never heard of his ever making any such pretensions [and] I dont think he ever did though he Seemed to be A well wisher."[42]

A "well wisher" but not fully invested in his family and friends' Calvinist faith; a drinker but only in moderation; a jokester and storyteller who could stand apart from his neighbors and friends enough to see and highlight their foibles; a farm laborer and rail-splitter, but only when he could not avoid it; a hard enough worker, but someone who would rather read a good book . . . Indiana's Abraham Lincoln was a young man who was at once in but not of his surroundings, who intimately knew Little Pigeon Creek but also managed to keep both it and its culture at arm's length. And by the time he was well into his teen years, he wanted to do more than this—he wanted to get out of Indiana.

LEAVING

L incoln visited William Wood's home again sometime in 1829. This time, however, he was not interested in borrowing newspapers or discussing the pros and cons of temperance. Instead, he "stood around, timid and shy," Wood recalled. "I knew he wanted something."

Finally, Lincoln spoke up. He understood that Wood had friends in the river trade along the Ohio, and he wanted a "recommendation to some boat," a crewman's position, so he could get away from Little Pigeon Creek. Wood was reluctant to help. "Abe, your age is against you," Wood replied, "you are not twenty-one yet." Leaving the farm before he attained the "age of majority" could get Abraham in trouble; legally, he was required to remain on his father's farm. "I know that, but I want a start," Lincoln insisted. Wood listened sympathetically but in the end decided against it "for the boy's good."[1]

Abraham was restive and very weary of life at the Lincoln farm. "One thing is true of him," Dennis Hanks emphasized, "he was ambitious." He had grown to realize that his family's little corner of Indiana was a dead end if he wanted to ever really make something of himself, peopled as it was largely by farmers who were not so very different from his father and seemed uninterested in much more than keeping dry roofs over their families' heads and bringing in good crops.[2]

He began looking for reasons to leave, if only for a short while. With his stepbrother, John, he went to Louisville, Kentucky, in 1827 and found work on the Louisville and Portland Canal, a long-standing project to create a two-mile bypass around the Falls of the Ohio River

near Louisville, the only major navigation obstacle on the river between Pittsburgh and New Orleans. Abraham and John were probably
day laborers, and the work was surely hard. But the pay was good, and
the two were compensated with silver dollars. "This is the first silver
dollar Lincoln ever had or owned," Augustus Chapman remembered,
"and of it he was very proud." Abraham quite likely had to give that
silver dollar to his father, along with the rest of any money he made on
his own. This may have been the unspoken context for his conversation with Wood: he wanted "a start" to be able to keep the money he
earned by the sweat of his own labor.[3]

Intellectually, he was moving beyond Indiana as well. He began to
evince a greater interest in national politics at about this time, talk-
ing current events with Wood and trying his hand at political writing—not just the temperance piece, but more directly civics-minded
musings. He "wrote a piece on national politics," Wood remembered,
"saying that the American government was the best form of government in the world for an intelligent people [and] that it ought to be
kept sound and preserved forever: that general education should [be]
fostered and carried all over the country: that the Constitution should
be saved the Union perpetuated and the laws revered." This essay has
since been lost, but it seems to have been echoed in themes Lincoln
voiced a few years later in one of his first major speeches before the
Young Men's Lyceum of Springfield, Illinois.[4]

People remembered him beginning to talk politics in general store
gatherings around the area. He also began to frequent local courthouses. This in itself was not unusual. Court day was a popular form
of entertainment in rural communities, a rare opportunity to leave
the farmwork drudgery and watch frontier barristers perform before
juries and the court. "The 'crowds' at that day thought the holding
of a court a great affair," according to one early Indiana lawyer, and
"the people came hundreds of miles to see the judges, and hear the
lawyers 'plead,' as they called it."[5]

Lincoln was enamored of courthouses. He was fascinated by the
proceedings and was especially enamored of a Hoosier attorney named
John Brackenridge, who enjoyed a high reputation in Lincoln's corner
of the state for his jury speechmaking. Lincoln also attended more

formal court days, once walking fifteen miles to the town of Boonville to watch the circuit court in session.[6]

Given his eventual career as an attorney, some believed long afterward that Lincoln quickly decided on a career in the law when he visited all these Indiana courthouses, but this was unlikely. The law would have held a particular fascination for him because it involved two activities he thoroughly enjoyed: reading and speechmaking. But watching various Hoosier lawyers "plead" was a long way from actually choosing the law as a career. Most lawyers, even the very rough-hewn backwoods "pettifoggers," possessed some form of education, and Lincoln was keenly aware that he had none.[7]

If he wanted out of Indiana, Lincoln was more likely to follow a river-related occupation, for he spent as much time on or near rivers as he did in courthouses. The Ohio continued to beckon. When Abraham crossed into Indiana in 1816, it had been a barrier; ten years later, it was an opportunity. At thirteen Abraham accompanied his cousin Dennis and a man named Squire Hall, who had married Abraham's stepsister Matilda, to Posey's Landing and cut cordwood on the river, which earned him pay not in money but in the material to make a brand new shirt, "the first white shirt he ever had in his life." He also helped a man named James Taylor operate a ferry at the mouth of the Anderson River, where it emptied into the Ohio. This job involved a considerable absence from home, as he lived with Taylor and his family for several months, not only operating the ferry but also helping grind corn at their mill and assisting some other local farmers as they slaughtered hogs—"rough work" for which he received thirty-one cents per day. This money also probably found its way into Thomas's pocket.[8]

Abraham lived with other families in the area as well, as often as he could: William Jones and his family in Gentryville, for whom Abraham worked and clerked in his store; another Jones family, who lived near the site of the future town of Dale, for whom he also worked in 1827; and the Grass family, who lived in Rockport. By 1828 he would have been a relatively rare presence at the Little Pigeon Creek farm.[9]

That year he hired out as a one-man crew on a flatboat for James Gentry, the merchant and entrepreneur who had founded the town of Gentryville near the Lincoln farm. Gentry was a man of some means who, along with many other Hoosiers of the day, used the Ohio River as a commercial highway to the Mississippi River and eventually New Orleans. It was common practice for farmers to load their excess produce onto homemade flatboats, make the long trek to New Orleans, and sell everything they could—even the flatboat— then book passage on a steamship home. Thomas Lincoln made at least two such trips himself when a young man living in Kentucky, though in his case the lack of steam-powered boats meant he had to walk all the way home.[10]

Now his son would do much the same, albeit James Gentry had agreed to pay his passage back to Indiana. The flatboat was operated by Gentry's son, Allen. The two young men pushed off for New Orleans sometime in the spring of 1828 and made their way down the Ohio and then out into the Mississippi. The trip was entirely uneventful, the pair stopping at intervals along the riverfront to barter and trade, until around midnight one evening at a place just north of New Orleans, they were suddenly awakened by "seven Negroes with intent to kill and rob them," as Lincoln later described it. One aimed a vicious blow with a wooden club at Lincoln's head just as he emerged from the boathouse; it caught him partially on the head but also partially glanced off the boathouse structure, deflecting its force. Gathering his wits, Gentry yelled, "Lincoln, get the guns and shoot!" This was pure bluff; they had no guns. But the thieves hastily vacated the boat, never to be seen again.[11]

Lincoln and Gentry continued on their way, landing in New Orleans and disposing of their cargo as expected, then returning home. It was quite the little adventure, the longest trip Lincoln made outside the immediate area around Little Pigeon Creek while he lived in Indiana. Despite the scare of the assault by the thieves—or maybe in a strange way because of it—it seems to have further whetted Lincoln's appetite for a life outside of Indiana; it was not long afterward that he approached Wood about possibly landing a boat crewman's position somewhere on the river.

His father was growing restless as well, if for different reasons. By 1830 Thomas was forty-two years old. With old age looming, and not much in the way of a viable plan for how he and Sarah would approach their sunset years, Thomas seems to have become uneasy regarding his long-term prospects in Indiana. Just getting by had worked well enough to that point, but Thomas had been able to do so in large part because he had so much help from his children, stepchildren, and other relatives such as Dennis Hanks. But they were all growing up now, starting their own families and pursuing their own priorities. Dennis would remain close, as would Thomas's stepson, John. But nearly everybody else had at least one foot out the cabin door.

This certainly included Abraham. While there is no record of any open conflict between this aging father and his fully grown son, Thomas had to have realized that Abraham wanted out, and sooner rather than later. All those jobs in Louisville and along the Ohio River, the long flatboat trip with Gentry to New Orleans, the extended stays with other families in the area—they veritably shouted "anywhere but here," as did the sullen looks Abraham likely gave his father as he continued to hand over his earnings. The young man would soon be gone, rarely, if ever, to return, and whatever emotional toll that may or may not have taken on Thomas, in practical terms it meant one less strong back to work the farm.

In the meantime, another Hanks relative, Dennis's cousin John, had moved into eastern Illinois and was urging other family members and friends to do the same. John had lived with the Lincolns in Indiana for four years, from 1823 until around 1827, working alongside Abraham and Dennis on the farm, "grubbing, hoeing, making fences, etc." John returned to Kentucky for a year and then moved with his wife, Susan, to Macon County, Illinois, in 1828. He was soon sending back glowing reports to his family about Illinois, including a letter to Thomas urging him to move there and make a fresh start.[12]

John's letter struck a chord with Thomas. Perhaps he came to believe that all he needed was just such a fresh start, one more new beginning. Dennis thought he was attracted by the rumors he heard, mostly from John Hanks, regarding the "rich prairies of Illinois already cleared and prepared for the plow." That last point was no small matter; Thomas thought the Illinois prairie was a bit more hospitable than Indiana's rolling, heavily wooded hills. A fresh outbreak of the "milk sickness" in the Little Pigeon Creek area likely added to Thomas's desire to relocate.[13]

He nevertheless seems to have hesitated before making the move, for at about this same time he began to construct a new cabin, a major project he surely would not have undertaken had his mind been irrevocably set on moving. The cabin would be his third while living in Indiana, on a hill not far from where their current dwelling stood and within a short walk from Nancy's gravesite. Abraham pitched in to help; Wood recalled encountering him felling a large tree at about this time, and when he asked the young man what he was doing, Abraham replied that "he was going to saw it into plank for his father's new house."[14]

That third cabin was never completed. At some point early in 1829 Thomas made up his mind once and for all and began preparations for the journey to Illinois. He sold hogs and corn to a nearby neighbor, and he sold his Indiana landholdings. He and Sarah also returned briefly to Elizabethtown to sell what was left of the property she still owned in that area, thinking perhaps they needed the money for the move and that relocation still farther westward to Illinois would finally sever their Kentucky connections. They cleared over $100 from the sale. Altogether Thomas managed to amass a considerable sum of cash, nearly $500, with which to finance their Illinois venture.[15]

They left Little Pigeon Creek in the early spring of 1830. It was a large party: Thomas, Sarah, and Abraham; Abraham's stepbrother, John; Dennis Hanks and his family; Squire Hall; and Abraham's stepsister Matilda and their children. They lumbered north- and westward, Abraham driving a wagon drawn by two oxen, loaded with furniture and other household goods, along with some livestock. The weather was still cold and the going slow, made difficult by rivers swollen with heavy rain and swampy areas covered in ice-cold water and sheets of ice. Crossing the Kaskaskia River in Illinois, they came very near losing the wagon and the oxen in the water and muck; the animals had to be lashed unmercifully by Abraham, "cutting open the hide." Making the crossing at last, Abraham saw his dog floundering and plunged back into the icy water to retrieve the stricken animal. "He got to the dog [and] took him, frightened nearly to death, in his long and strong arms, [and] carried him to the wagon," recalled a friend to whom Lincoln later related the tale, "the dog [crouching] close to Mrs. Lincoln's feet, scared half out of his wits. . . . After the family had crossed and got on dry land Abe found difficulty in getting the dog out of the wagon."[16]

His twenty-first birthday—the age of majority and his legal freedom—came and went in February 1830. Despite his burning desire to strike out on his own, Abraham remained with his family throughout the trek to Illinois and for some time afterward, helping Thomas and Dennis construct yet another cabin. He also helped build a rail fence to enclose the first few acres Thomas planned to cultivate, and he worked at the usual variety of odd jobs around his family's new neighborhood. For a time he lived a life of farming and farm labor that did not look so very different from his life in Indiana.[17]

But nothing went right for Thomas in Illinois. During the summer he and Sarah were struck with what was locally referred to as the "ague," debilitating bouts of fever and chills that were likely malarial, transmitted by the swarms of mosquitoes blanketing the area. The following winter of 1830–31 was the stuff of legend, ever after referred to in Illinois lore as the "winter of the deep snow," with successive blizzards that buried the state under sometimes as much as three feet of snow. "There was great suffering among the people," read an early history of Illinois; their crops were destroyed, "a great deal of their stock died, [and] the wild hogs, deer and other animals in the forests were nearly swept out of existence."[18]

Thomas was so discouraged that he decided to pack up and return home to Indiana—a desperate and puzzling move, given that he had long since sold all his Indiana land. They made it as far as Coles County, Illinois, where they lingered with relatives and friends who had settled in the area, even going so far as to construct a cabin, where they remained until 1834.[19]

By then Abraham was long gone.

EPILOGUE

Lincoln had no intention of accompanying Thomas and Sarah in their headlong retreat back to Indiana. As they prepared to leave in March 1831, Abraham packed his belongings and struck out in the opposite direction, walking generally west into central Illinois, even as his father and stepmother headed south and east.

As it happened, Thomas and Sarah never returned to Indiana. They moved around in several places throughout Coles County, Illinois, eventually settling for good in an area called Goosenest Prairie. Thomas scuffled about, laboring much as he had always done at farming, mill-work, and other odd jobs. He died from an unidentified kidney disease in 1851. Sarah outlasted both her husband and her stepson; when William Herndon interviewed her in the fall of 1865, four years before her death, she was a frail seventy-six years of age but still of a relatively sound mind and full of memories regarding her now famous stepson. "Abe was the best boy I ever saw or expect to see," she told Herndon, then added sadly, "I wish I had died when my husband died."[1]

Lincoln did not return to Indiana until fourteen years later, when he made a month-long political trip speaking on behalf of Whig candidates and policies in the fall of 1844, just before the November elections. Exactly where he went and how many speeches he delivered are matters of conjecture; he certainly spoke in Rockport and possibly also in the Indiana towns of Vincennes, Washington, and Bruceville. Only the content of the Rockport speech survives, standard fare for Lincoln the Whig politician and lawyer, in which he "pointed out the advantages of a Protective Tariff" in what one newspaper correspondent described as a speech that "was plain, argumentative, and of an hour's duration."[2]

His 1844 Indiana trip was not just about business; he also found the time to visit Spencer County, where he paid his respects at his mother's grave. The site evoked melancholy in the now successful thirty-five-year-old lawyer, husband, and father—a man far removed from the boy who had helped haul his mother's body to the crest of that hill for burial.

Lincoln chose to express his sorrow in verse. With an apt invocation of the mixed feelings his time in Indiana aroused, the poem read in part:

> My childhood home I see again,
> And sadden with the view;
> And still, as memory crowds my brain,
> There's pleasure in it too.

Yet in the end, Lincoln's poem was more heavily weighted toward the sadness:

> How changed, as time has sped!
> Young childhood grown, strong manhood gray,
> And half of all are dead. . . .
> Till every sound appears a knell,
> And every spot a grave.
> I range the fields with pensive tread,
> And pace the hollow rooms,
> And feel (companion of the dead)
> I'm living in the tombs.[3]

On that note, he left Little Pigeon Creek, never to return. "I would much like to visit the old home, and old friends of my boyhood," he wrote to an Indiana friend during the presidential election of 1860, "but I fear the chance for doing so soon, is not very good."[4]

Lincoln returned to Indiana four more times. In 1849 he made a brief and uneventful trip across the state and back, on his way to Washington, DC, to seek political support and favors from the new administration of Whig president Zachary Taylor, for whom he had vigorously campaigned. Ten years later he was in Indianapolis, speaking on behalf of the Republican Party in advance of the upcoming presidential election. His speech was subsequently dominated by sectional politics and slavery. But he opened as any good politician might, referencing briefly his Hoosier connections with no apparent emotion other than a bit of humor, noting that "when he was in his eighth year, his father brought him over from the neighboring state of Kentucky, and settled in the State of Indiana, and he grew up to his present enormous height on our own good soil of Indiana." The audience laughed.[5]

During his third Indiana visit, the mood was considerably less jocular. The day before his fifty-second birthday in February 1861, president-elect Lincoln left Springfield, Illinois, by train for Washington, DC, with the nation he now led in the process of disintegration. He arrived at the Indiana state line a little after noon, and from there until his arrival at the state border in Cincinnati the next day, he made a series of public appearances before anxious crowds at Lafayette, Thornton, Lebanon, Indianapolis, Morris, Shelbyville, Greensburg, and Lawrenceburg—an exhausting tour across a part of the state that had been little more than a howling wilderness when Lincoln arrived as a boy forty-five years previously.

His overnight stay in Indianapolis was particularly grueling: artillery salutes and bands, two speeches from the balcony of his hotel room in the Bates House downtown (though his second speech was simply an announcement that he "had no speech to make" and the wry observation that if he heeded every single call for an address to the crowds he was encountering, he would be late for his own inauguration), a meal with the governor the next morning, a meeting with state legislators and other dignitaries at the capitol building, and yet another speech from the hotel balcony an hour before he left the city. Everywhere there were crowds; an estimated twenty thousand people escorted him from his train to the hotel, where three thousand people somehow managed to cram themselves into the parlor.[6]

His speeches as president-elect were understandably national and not local in content and focus, his mind on what was occurring in

Washington, DC, and south of the Mason-Dixon Line. Already the new president was becoming the nation's man, belonging to the United States more than Indiana, Kentucky, or Illinois. "I suppose you are all Union men here," he told the audience at Lawrenceburg, a small town just north and west of Cincinnati, where Indiana and Ohio converge, "and I suppose that you are in favor of doing full justice to all, whether on that side of the river," and here he pointed to the Ohio River, "or on your own." They answered with cries of "We are!" Lincoln likely nodded in agreement. After a few concluding remarks, he boarded the train and continued his long trip east.[7]

His fourth and final visit to Indiana was the gloomiest of them all and irrefutable proof that he now belonged to the nation, indeed the world. Sixteen days after Lincoln was assassinated at Ford's Theatre in Washington, DC, his body arrived in Indianapolis, in a special funeral train that had been making its way across the United States, with massive crowds of mourners lining the tracks and gathering in the towns and cities along the way. Each town tried to surpass the others in its expressions of grief and respect for their fallen leader: black cloth and crepe were draped over windows and doorways, and archways were constructed with black materials and flowers. In the larger cities of New York, Albany, Buffalo, Cleveland, and Columbus, the coffin was removed and placed on a dais or an ornate catafalque, open for viewing by hundreds of thousands of people. An estimated one out of every four Americans viewed Lincoln's body or at least glimpsed the funeral train as it passed slowly by. "The thing had become half circus, half heartbreak," noted one sardonic observer.[8]

Indianapolis was the train's primary Indiana destination, and the city's leaders did not want to be outdone in paying respects to what many in the state regarded as a native son. When the funeral train chugged into town early on Sunday morning, April 30, it was greeted by yet another immense crowd, braving a cold drizzle to escort the coffin from the train station to the platform erected under the state house dome for public viewing. There it remained until midnight, seen by an estimated fifty thousand people, before being placed back aboard the train for the journey to Lafayette and Michigan

City on the state line, thence to Chicago and its final destination of Springfield, Illinois.[9]

Lincoln would be laid to rest in Springfield, his hometown in many ways, and honored by monuments, statues, and plaques all over the United States. Nearly everyone who had come into even brief contact with the man would over the ensuing years claim their little bit of fame and immortality by highlighting the fact. But Indiana had a stronger claim than most. As that funeral train left the state, an Indianapolis newspaper stated with some satisfaction, "Every Indianian may feel the honor of the State has been rather brightened than compromised by their reception of the remains of President Lincoln, and that State where he passed some years of his youth, has rendered her full quota of honor to him as the Savior of his Country."[10]

ACKNOWLEDGMENTS

I have always made it a point to begin the acknowledgments section of any book I write about Abraham Lincoln by recognizing the debt I owe to my advisor and mentor, the late Phillip S. Paludan. I still keenly feel his influence: his passion for the Civil War era, his thoroughness and attention to detail, and perhaps most of all his unwillingness to substitute hagiographic platitudes for critical thinking, especially where Lincoln studies are concerned. He is missed.

Sylvia Rodrigue has been a wonderful editor and friend while working with me on this book and quite a few other projects; her patience and dedication, as well as her top-notch editing skills, make working with her a real pleasure. Richard Etulain has also been a most enthusiastic and supportive editor and advisor. Additionally, I thank the editors of the Papers of Abraham Lincoln and the anonymous peer reviewers, who gave this manuscript a thorough and insightful reading; my copy editor, Joyce Bond; and Amy Alsip and the other highly skilled (and patient) members of the Southern Illinois University Press staff. They all saved me from numerous errors and gaffes. Any remaining mistakes in the manuscript are entirely my own.

I have long benefited from the wisdom and friendship of William Bartelt, who wrote an excellent book on Lincoln's Indiana days and has always been generous with advice and support. Mike Capps, chief interpreter at the Lincoln Boyhood Home in Lincoln City, Indiana, has also been very supportive and graciously shared with me his impressive knowledge of the Lincoln farm and Lincoln's Hoosier upbringing. In securing illustrations for this book, I was ably assisted by the staff of the archives at Lincoln Memorial University, particularly Travis Souther, archivist and special collections librarian.

Anderson University has provided me with a congenial environment, where I have been privileged to teach now for over eighteen years. Dan Allen, Michael Frank, David Murphy, Jaye Rogers, and Joel Schrock are my colleagues in the Department of History and Political Science, but more than that, they are also all my good friends. Jill Branscum of the Interlibrary Loan Department at Anderson

University's Nicholson Library as always provided me with indispensable help in procuring sometimes obscure items for my research; and Jan Brewer, the director of library services, has likewise been a valuable friend and ally. Our department's administrative assistant, Janice Bell, provided both important assistance and a sympathetic ear as I worked through the various ups and downs of this project. I must also thank my students, particularly those who attended my courses on the American Civil War and historical methodology and patiently endured my classroom ramblings regarding Lincoln, Indiana, and history generally.

My wife, Julie, is my long-standing pillar of love and support, as are my children, Nathan and Rachel, and my stepchildren, Brad (and his wife, Charlotte), Chris, and Evan. I also cannot neglect my cat, Ella, whom I have thanked in previous books for periodically wreaking kitty havoc by lying on my computer keyboard at most inopportune moments. She is older now, and considerably fatter, but this simply means that she is able to press more keys and is less easily dislodged. There are worse ways to grow old, I suppose.

NOTES

Prologue

1. The three autobiographies are Lincoln, "Brief Autobiography" (written for the compiler of the *Dictionary of Congress*), June [15?] 1858, in *The Collected Works of Abraham Lincoln*, ed. Roy P. Basler (New Brunswick, NJ: Rutgers University Press, 1953; hereafter *CW*), 2:459; "To Jesse W. Fell, Enclosing Autobiography," December 20, 1859, ibid., 3:511–12; and "Autobiography Written for John L. Scripps," c. June 1860, ibid., 4:60–68.
2. William H. Herndon and Jesse W. Weik, *Herndon's Lincoln* (1889; repr., Urbana: University of Illinois Press, 2006), 15.
3. Ibid., xxi (italics in original).
4. "To Jesse W. Fell, Enclosing Autobiography," December 20, 1859, *CW* 3:511.

1. Beginnings

1. The river is referred to in some contemporary accounts as "Anderson's River." See R. Gerald McMurtry, "The Lincoln Migration from Kentucky to Indiana," *Indiana Magazine of History* 33 (December 1937): 385.
2. John Woods, *Two Years' Residence in the Settlement on the English Prairie, in the Illinois Country, United States* (London: A. and R. Spottiswoode, 1822), 120; on the mill site, see Ward Hill Lamon, *The Life of Abraham Lincoln from His Birth to His Inauguration as President* (Bedford, MA: Applewood Books, 1872), 23.
3. Lamon, *Life of Abraham Lincoln*, 23; timber description in John Scott, *The Indiana Gazetteer*, 2nd ed. (Indianapolis: Douglas and Maguire, 1833), 163; it was an area called the "pocket," referenced in J. W. Wartmann to William H. Herndon, July 21, 1865, in Douglas L. Wilson and Rodney O. Davis, eds., *Herndon's Informants: Letters, Interviews, and Statements about Abraham Lincoln* (Urbana: University of Illinois Press, 1998; hereafter *HI*), 78; see also Arvil S. Barr, "A History of Warrick County, Indiana, Prior to 1820, Including a Sketch of Methodism in the County down to 1850" (master's thesis, University of Indiana, 1915), 16–19; on the exact date of the Lincolns' arrival, see McMurtry, "Lincoln Migration," 392.
4. On this point, see McMurtry's excellent examination in "Lincoln Migration," 391–93.
5. One tradition has Thomas Lincoln making an earlier trip in a flatboat loaded with whiskey and his carpentry tools, only to lose the whiskey

when the raft overturned; see, e.g., Arthur E. Morgan, "New Light on Lincoln's Boyhood," *Atlantic Monthly* 125 (February 1920): 208–10; but McMurtry, "Lincoln Migration," 390, has cast doubts on the veracity of this story; see also Joseph H. Barrett, *Life of Abraham Lincoln* (Cincinnati: Moore, Wilstach, and Baldwin, 1864).

6. Nathaniel Grigsby, interview with William H. Herndon, September 12, 1865, *HI*, 111; John Hanks, interview with John Miles, ibid., 5; A. H. Chapman to William H. Herndon, September 8, 1865, ibid., 97; Dennis F. Hanks to William H. Herndon, c. December 1865, ibid., 149.

7. John Hanks, interview with John Miles, *HI*, 5, and interview with Herndon, c. 1865–66, ibid., 454; see also Dennis F. Hanks, Interview with William H. Herndon, June 13, 1865, ibid., 37, and Nathaniel Grigsby to William H. Herndon, September 4, 1865, ibid., 94, 113; David Turnham to William H. Herndon, November 19, 1866, ibid., 403. I have followed their line of thinking in their physical description, since it seems to represent something of a consensus, though it should be noted that one person, Samuel Haycraft, described Nancy as "heavy"; see Haycraft to William H. Herndon, c. June 1865, ibid., 67.

8. Nathaniel Grigsby, interview with William H. Herndon, September 12, 1865, *HI*, 113; Elizabeth Crawford, interview with William H. Herndon, September 16th, 1865, ibid., 126; John Hanks, interview with William H. Herndon, c. 1865–66, ibid., 456; David Turnham, interview with William H. Herndon, September 15, 1865, ibid., 122. See also John Hanks to Jesse W. Weik, June 12, 1887, ibid., 615, in which he seems to be describing Lincoln's sister, though this is not entirely clear; his description is in concordance with others that Sarah was dark-haired, had a dark complexion, and was "hevey [*sic*] built."

9. David Turnham, interview with William H. Herndon, September 15, 1865, *HI*, 121; John Hanks to Jesse W. Weik, June 12, 1887, ibid., 615; Anna Caroline Gentry, interview with William H. Herndon, September 17, 1865, *HI*, 131; for an adult description of him as "gawky," see Joshua F. Speed to William H. Herndon, c. 1882, ibid., 588.

10. Frances Fisher Browne, *The Everyday Life of Abraham Lincoln* (1886; repr., Lincoln: University of Nebraska Press, 1995), 50–51.

11. See L. C. Rudolph, "The Settlers," in Ralph D. Gray, ed., *Indiana History: A Book of Readings* (Bloomington: Indiana University Press, 1994), 96; and Barbara J. Steinson, "Rural Life in Indiana, 1800–1950," *Indiana Magazine of History* 90 (September 1994): 220.

12. Thomas Jefferson, *Notes on the State of Virginia* (New York: Palgrave, 2002), 12.

13. Lincoln, "To Jesse W. Fell, Enclosing Autobiography," December 20, 1859, *CW* 3:511.

14. Numbers here are from "United States Resident Population by State: 1790–1850," U.S. Censuses of Population and Housing, New Jersey Department of Labor and Workforce Development, http://lwd.dol .state.nj.us/labor/lpa/census/1990/poptrd1.htm, accessed August 3, 2015.

15. The origins and meaning of the name Hoosiers are unclear; see William E. Wilson, *Indiana: A History* (Bloomington: Indiana University Press, 1966), 12–13; Edward E. Moore, comp., *Moore's Hoosier Cyclopedia* (Indianapolis: Press of Wm. B. Burford, 1905), 276; and Ronald L. Baker, *Hoosier Folk Legends* (Bloomington: Indiana University Press, 1982), 172–73.

16. Otho Winger, *History of the Church of the Brethren in Indiana* (Elgin, IL: Brethren Publishing House, 1917), 21.

17. Population data from "Resident Population and Apportionment of the U.S. House of Representatives: Indiana," U.S. Census Bureau, https:// www.census.gov/dmd/www/resapport/states/indiana.pdf, accessed July 25, 2015; Corydon description and quote in Charles Moores, "Old Corydon," *Indiana Magazine of History* 13 (March 1917): 21.

18. Wilson, *Indiana*, 82; Lincoln, "To Jesse W. Fell, Enclosing Autobiography," December 20, 1859, *CW* 3:511; William Monroe Cockrum, *Pioneer History of Indiana: Including Stories, Incidents, and Customs of the Early Settlers* (Oakland City, IN: Press of Oakland City, 1907), 503.

19. James Leander Scott, *A Journal of a Missionary Tour through Pennsylvania, Ohio, Indiana, Illinois, Iowa, Wiskonsin, and Michigan* (Providence, RI: J. L. Scott, 1843), 72.

20. Mary M. Crawford, ed., "Mrs. Lydia B. Bacon's Journal, 1811–1812," *Indiana Magazine of History* 40 (December 1944): 373–74.

21. "'Indiana,' by John Campbell," Indiana University Bloomington Libraries, http://libraries.iub.edu/indiana-john-campbell, accessed July 24, 2015.

22. See, generally, Bert Anson, *The Miami Indians* (Norman: University of Oklahoma Press, 1970).

23. Elizabeth Glenn and Stewart Rafert, *The Native Americans* (Indianapolis: Indiana Historical Society Press, 2009); Barr, "History of Warrick County, Indiana," 3–4.

24. Robert M. Taylor and Connie A. McBirney, *Peopling Indiana: The Ethnic Experience* (Indianapolis: Indiana Historical Society, 1996), 83; Gregory S. Rose, "The Distribution of Indiana's Ethnic and Racial Minorities in 1850," *Indiana Magazine of History* 87 (September 1991): 224; William E. Wilson, *The Angel and the Serpent: The Story of New Harmony* (Bloomington: Indiana University Press, 1964); Crawford, "Mrs. Lydia B. Bacon's Journal," 370.

25. See James H. Madison, *The Indiana Way: A State History* (Bloomington: Indiana University Press, 1986), 59–60.

26. Rose, "Distribution of Indiana's Ethnic and Racial Minorities," 238–39; John V. H. Dippel, *Race to the Frontier: "White Flight" and Westward Expansion* (New York: Algora Pub., 2005), 122–125.

27. Wilson, *Indiana*, 68–73; Madison, *Indiana Way*, 116–17.

28. Herald letter available in Frank E. Stevens, "Illinois in the War of 1812–1814," in *Transactions of the Illinois State Historical Society for the Year 1904* (Springfield, IL: Phillips Bros., 1904), 100.

29. Ronald J. Drez, *The War of 1812, Conflict and Deception* (Baton Rouge: Louisiana State University Press, 2014), 97; William Henry Harrison to William Eustis, April 22 and 29, 1812, in *Indiana Historical Collections*, vol. 9: *Governor's Messages and Letters*, vol. 2, ed. Logan Esarey (Indianapolis: Indiana Historical Commission, 1922), 41–42.

30. Crawford, "Mrs. Lydia B. Bacon's Journal," 377.

31. William Faux, *Memorable Days in America* (1823; repr., Carlisle, PA: Applewood Books, 2007), 199; Lincoln, "Autobiography Written for John L. Scripps," *CW* 4:62.

32. Steinson, "Rural Life in Indiana," 220–24; Paul Salstrom, *From Pioneering to Persevering: Family Farming in Indiana to 1880* (Lafayette, IN: Purdue University Press, 2007), 3–4; Clarence H. Danhof, *Changes in Agriculture: The Northern United States, 1820–1870* (Cambridge, MA: Harvard University Press, 1969), 123–24.

33. Salstrom, *From Pioneering to Persevering*, 5–6, 43–45.

34. Thomas Jefferson, *The Writings of Thomas Jefferson*, ed. H. A. Washington (New York: Derby, 1861), 8:405–6.

35. *History of Fayette County, Indiana* (Chicago: Warner, Beers and Co., 1886), 40.

36. Steinson, "Rural Life in Indiana," 205–10.

37. Salstrom, *From Pioneering to Persevering*, 3.

38. See, generally, Robert P. Swierenga, "Land Speculation and Its Impact on American Economic Growth and Welfare: A Historiographical Review," *Western Historical Quarterly* 8 (July 1977): 283–302; Aaron M. Sakolski, *The Great American Land Bubble: The Amazing Story of Land-Grabbing, Speculations, and Booms from Colonial Days to the Present Time* (1932; repr., New York: Martino, 2011); George E. Lewis, *The Indiana Land Company, 1763–1798: A Study in Eighteenth-Century Frontier Land Speculation and Business Venture* (Glendale, CA: Arthur H. Clark Co., 1941).

39. Sandford C. Cox, *Recollections of the Early Settlement of the Wabash Valley* (Lafayette, IN: Courier, 1860), 18; see also Logan Esarey, *A History of Indiana, from Its Exploration to 1850*, vol. 1 (Indianapolis: B. F. Bowen, 1918), 395–98.

40. *Biographical and Historical Record of Kosciusko County, Indiana* (Chicago: Lewis Pub. Co., 1887), 490.

41. William Wesley Woollen, *Biographical and Historical Sketches of Early Indiana* (Indianapolis: Hammond and Co., 1883), 426; Benjamin Cothen Cressy, *An Appeal in Behalf of the Indiana Theological Seminary, Located at South Hanover, Indiana* (Boston: Pierce and Parker, 1832), 11 (italics in original).

42. Oliver Hampton Smith, *Early Indiana Trials and Sketches: Reminiscences by Hon. O. H. Smith* (Cincinnati: Moore, Wilstach, Keys and Co., 1858), 5.

43. Henry William Ellsworth, *Valley of the Upper Wabash, Indiana, with Hints on Its Agricultural Advantages* (New York: Pratt, Robinson, and Co., 1838), viii.

44. Cox, *Recollections*, 16.

45. Scott, *Journal of a Missionary Tour*, 70.

46. Samuel Roosevelt Johnson, *O Worship the Lord in the Beauty of Holiness: A Sermon at the Consecration of St. Mary's Church, Delphi, Indiana* (New York: Stanford and Swords, 1845), 10 (italics in original).

47. Thomas C. Searle, "Dutch Settlement in Indiana," *The Christian Spectator* 2 (November; New Haven: Howe and Spalding, 1820), 610.

48. Daniel Fanshaw, *Twenty-First Annual Report of the American Tract Society* (New York: American Tract Society, 1846), 107.

49. Isaac Kinley, "Education of the Farmer," in *Second Annual Report of the Indiana State Board of Agriculture* (Indianapolis: J. P. Chapman, 1853), 362.

50. On newspapers in this era, see, generally, Edward Pessen, *Jacksonian America: Society, Personality, and Politics* (Urbana: University of Illinois Press, 1985), 63–64.

51. Indiana Constitution (1816), Art. 6, Sec. 1, Indiana Historical Bureau, http://www.in.gov/history/2877.htm, accessed August 29, 2015; Cox, *Recollections*, 17.

2. Roots

1. William Dean Howells, *Life of Abraham Lincoln* (Springfield, IL: Abraham Lincoln Assoc., 1938), 18; Lincoln to Solomon Lincoln, March 6, 1848, *CW* 1:456.

2. Bradley R. Hoch, *The Lincoln Trail in Pennsylvania: A History and Guide* (University Park: Pennsylvania State University Press, 2001), 25.

3. Lincoln, "To Jesse W. Fell, Enclosing Autobiography," December 20, 1859, *CW* 3:511; "Autobiography Written for John L. Scripps," c. June 1860, ibid., 4:60.

4. See Ida Tarbell's older but still seminal study, *Abraham Lincoln and His Ancestors* (New York: Harper and Bros., 1924), 55–57.

5. Dennis Hanks, interview with William H. Herndon, June 13, 1865, *HI*, 36; also A. H. Chapman, written statement, September 8, 1865, ibid., 96.

Chapman's account must be treated with caution, as it contains numerous factual errors and inconsistencies, but I have used elements from his statement when they are consistent with what Hanks said.

6. A. H. Chapman, written statement, September 8, 1865, *HI*, 96. As I indicated above, I believe Chapman's account should be treated with caution, but his claims about Mordecai are corroborated by another source, William Clagett, written statement, c. February 1866, ibid., 220.

7. Herndon and Weik, *Herndon's Lincoln*, 2–3; while Herndon here spelled her name "Lucy," the more commonly used spelling was "Lucey" Hanks.

8. See https://www.familytreedna.com/public/HanksDNAProject/default.aspx?section=news, accessed October 19, 2016; I am very grateful to Richard G. Hileman, one of the directors of this study, for making me aware of it.

9. See Lincoln, "Autobiography Written for John L. Scripps," c. June 1860, *CW* 4:61.

10. Oliver Fraysse, *Lincoln, Land, and Labor: 1809–1860* (Urbana: University of Illinois Press, 1988), 9–10; Lowell H. Harrison, *Lincoln of Kentucky* (Lexington: University Press of Kentucky, 2000), 23; Brian R. Dirck, *Lincoln the Lawyer* (Urbana: University of Illinois Press, 2007), 14–15.

11. Anonymous letter written to *Maryland Journal*, April 4, 1786, quoted in Lowell H. Harrison, *Kentucky's Road to Statehood* (Lexington: University Press of Kentucky, 1992), 16.

12. Frederick Law Olmstead, *The Cotton Kingdom: A Traveler's Observations on Cotton and Slavery in the American Slave States* (New York: Mason Bros., 1862), 116.

13. Lincoln, "Autobiography Written for John L. Scripps," c. June 1860, *CW* 4:61.

14. See Brian R. Dirck, *Abraham Lincoln and White America* (Lawrence: University Press of Kansas, 2012), 18.

15. He may have made anywhere from one to possibly three such trips; see McMurtry, "Lincoln Migration," 391; Dennis F. Hanks, interview with William H. Herndon, June 13, 1865, *HI*, 38. A. H. Chapman claims that Lincoln brought whiskey and a store of goods with him on this trip, storing these belongings with an acquaintance named Francis Posey; see Chapman, written statement, September 8, 1865, *HI*, 98. But McMurtry, ibid., 390–91, casts doubt on the idea of his bringing whiskey into Indiana, as well as other aspects of this story.

16. Dennis Hanks, interview with William H. Herndon, June 13, 1865, *HI*, 39; "fast failing" quote from Thomas L. D. Johnston, interview with William H. Herndon, c. 1866, ibid., 532.

17. I am grateful to Lincoln Boyhood Home historian Michael Capps for guiding me in understanding this route and the placement of the spring.

18. Nathaniel Grigsby, interview with William H. Herndon, September 12, 1865, *HI*, 111.

19. Dennis Hanks, interview with William H. Herndon, June 13, 1865, *HI*, 39; Lincoln, "Autobiography Written for John L. Scripps," c. June 1860, *CW* 4:62. The typical "two-face camp" in Indiana is described in some detail in Logan Esarey, *The Indiana Home* (Bloomington: Indiana University Press, 1953), 25.

20. Dennis Hanks, interview with Erasmus Wright, June 8, 1865, *HI*, 28. An interview Herndon conducted with four of Lincoln's Little Pigeon Creek neighbors does mention a chimney at the cabin's "East end," but it is not clear exactly which of several Lincoln homes is being discussed here; see Nathaniel Grigsby, Silas Richardson, Nancy Richardson, and John Romine, interview with William H. Herndon, September 14, 1865, ibid., 116.

21. Dennis Hanks, interview with William H. Herndon, June 13, 1865, *HI*, 39; see also Dennis F. Hanks, interview with Erastus Wright, June 8, 1865, ibid., 27–28.

22. Lincoln, "Autobiography Written for John L. Scripps," c. June 1860, *CW* 4:62; Dennis Hanks, interview with William H. Herndon, June 13, 1865, *HI*, 39.

23. Dennis Hanks, interview with William H. Herndon, June 13, 1865, *HI*, 39–40.

24. Nathaniel Grigsby, Silas Richardson, Nancy Richardson, and John Romine, interview with William H. Herndon, September 14, 1865, *HI*, 116; Dennis F. Hanks to William H. Herndon, January 6, 1866, ibid., 154.

25. *History of Warrick, Spencer, and Perry Counties, Indiana* (Chicago: Goodspeed Bros., 1885), 272–73, 366.

26. By way of comparison, Jesse W. Weik, *Weik's History of Putnam County, Indiana* (Indianapolis: B. F. Bowen, 1910), 143, describes an Indiana farmer who was able to clear about three acres at around the same time.

27. Maximilian Wied, *Travels in the Interior of North America* (London: Ackerman and Co., 1843), 481; *History of Miami County, Indiana* (Chicago: Brant and Fuller, 1887), 363.

28. On the practice of burning away underbrush, see *History of Miami County*, 363–64; Weik, *History of Putnam County*, 143; Andrew White Young, *History of Wayne County, Indiana, from Its First Settlement to the Present Time* (Cincinnati: Robert Clarke and Co., 1872), 37.

29. Stanley Coulter, *Forest Trees of Indiana* (Indianapolis: Wm. B. Burford, 1892), 6, 12–16.

30. Young, *History of Wayne County*, 37–38.

31. "D.L.," "A Plan to Remove Stumps," in *The Western Farmer and Gardener, Devoted to Agriculture, Horticulture, and Rural Economy*, vol. 2,

From October, 1840, to September, 1841, ed. Thomas Affleck (Cincinnati: Charles Foster, 1841), 251; "Patents Issued, with Remarks," in *Journal of the Franklin Institute of the State of Pennsylvania*, ed. Thomas P. Jones (Philadelphia: J. Harding, 1835), 94.

32. On the difficulties a first-season farmer might face, see Esarey, *Indiana Home*, 29.

33. On this process of "deadening," see James Flint, *Letters from America* (London: Longman, Hurst, Reese, Orme, and Brown, 1822), 313.

34. Young, *History of Wayne County*, 38.

35. Esarey, *Indiana Home*, 74.

36. On the central role of women in farmwork and farm production in nineteenth-century America, see Nancy Grey Osterud, *Bonds of Community: The Lives of Farm Women in Nineteenth-Century New York* (Ithaca, NY: Cornell University Press, 1991); and Osterud's useful (if somewhat out of the Lincolns' time period) essay, "'She Helped Me Hay It as Good as a Man': Relations among Women and Men in an Agricultural Community," in *"To Toil the Livelong Day": America's Women at Work, 1780–1980*, ed. Carol Groneman and Mary Beth Norton (Ithaca, NY: Cornell University Press, 1987), 87–97; on the commonality of women and children's farmwork, see Richard A. Easterlin, George Alter, and Gretchen A. Condran, "Farms and Farm Families in Old and New Areas: The Northern States in 1860," in *Family and Population in Nineteenth Century America*, ed. Tamara K. Hareven and Maris A. Vinovskis (Princeton, NJ: Princeton University Press, 1978), 67–68.

37. Paul M. Angle, ed., *The Lincoln Reader* (New York: DaCapo Press, 1946), 11–12, quotes Carl Sandburg in offering quite detailed descriptions of Thomas Lincoln's plowing in Kentucky, including his use of a plow "shod with iron," but the precise primary sourcing here is unclear, suggesting that this was generalization from known practices of Kentucky farmers at the time. Also quite useful is Henry G. Waltmann, *Pioneer Farming in Indiana: Thomas Lincoln's Major Crops* (Washington, DC: Smithsonian Institution, 1975), 23.

38. Dennis F. Hanks, interview with William H. Herndon, June 13, 1865, *HI*, 39, declares that Thomas had no "dogs—cats—hogs—cows—chickens or such like domestic animals." But Thomas did possess two horses, indicated by Hanks himself elsewhere, so it is quite possible Hanks had a lapse in memory here.

39. See the excellent and very meticulous discussion of Lincoln's corn crop planting in Waltmann, *Pioneer Farming in Indiana*, 6–26; Salstrom, *From Pioneering to Persevering*, 38–39; *History of Warrick, Spencer, and Perry Counties*, 293–94; Esarey, *Indiana Home*, 29–33.

40. Waltmann, *Pioneer Farming in Indiana*, 6–26.
41. Dennis F. Hanks, interview with William H. Herndon, June 13, 1865, *HI*, 40.
42. On the medical treatments common to frontier farms of the day, see John C. Gunn, *Gunn's Domestic Medicine; or, Poor Man's Friend*, 13th ed. (Pittsburgh: J. Edwards, 1839); Esarey, *Indiana Home*, 35.
43. Dennis F. Hanks, interview with William H. Herndon, June 13, 1865, *HI*, 39.

3. Mothers

1. Waltmann, *Pioneer Farming in Indiana*, 6, 86–88.
2. Dennis Hanks, interview with William H. Herndon, June 13, 1865, *HI*, 40; and interview dated September 8, 1865, ibid., 104.
3. Dirck, *Lincoln and White America*, 34.
4. Dennis Hanks, interview with William H. Herndon, September 8, 1865, *HI*, 105.
5. A. H. Chapman, written statement, September 8, 1865, *HI*, 98; Waltmann, *Pioneer Farming in Indiana*, 6.
6. Dennis Hanks, interview with Erastus Wright, June 8, 1865, *HI*, 27; interview with William H. Herndon, June 13, 1865, ibid., 37; and interview with Jesse W. Weik, c. 1886, ibid., 598; A. H. Chapman, written statement, September 8, 1865, ibid., 97; John Hanks, interview with William H. Herndon, c. 1865–66, ibid., 454.
7. Esarey, *Indiana Home*, 30–33.
8. "Laboring woman" quote in David Turnham to William H. Herndon, November 19, 1866, *HI*, 403; on Nancy's weaving, see Dennis Hanks, interview with William H. Herndon, June 13, 1865, ibid., 37.
9. Esarey, *Indiana Home*, 33; Waltmann, *Pioneer Farming in Indiana*, 69; Young, *History of Wayne County*, 36; see also Branson L. Harris, *Some Recollections of My Boyhood* (Indianapolis: Hollenbeck Press, 1900), 6–7.
10. Sereno Edwards Todd, *The Young Farmer's Manual* (New York: F. W. Woodward, 1867), 24; on the vital role of women in the farming economy of the day and their often invisible roles in a male-oriented society, see Joan M. Jensen, *Loosening the Bonds: Mid-Atlantic Farm Women, 1750–1850* (New Haven, CT: Yale University Press, 1986), 114–18.
11. Dennis Hanks, interview with William H. Herndon, June 13, 1865, *HI*, 36, hinted at some darker cause, suggesting that their lack of any more children was caused by "a private matter"; it is possible Nancy may have been unable to bear any more children because of some physical difficulty, but there is no evidence of this, other than Hanks's unexplained hint.

12. "Mr. Holmes," excerpt from the Maine *Farmer*, "Culture of Roots, Silk, etc.," *American Railroad Journal, and Advocate of Internal Improvements* 5 (1836): 520.

13. A. H. Chapman, written statement, September 8, 1865, *HI*, 97.

14. Zebedee was the father of James and John, two of Jesus's disciples. Dennis Hanks, interview with William H. Herndon, June 13, 1865, *HI*, 37.

15. Ibid.; the text of the deed is from Kent Masterson Brown, "Report on the Title of Thomas Lincoln to, and the History of, the Lincoln Boyhood Home along Knob Creek in LaRue County, Kentucky," https://archive.org/stream/reportontitleoft00brow/reportontitleoft00brow_djvu.txt, accessed October 21, 2015.

16. Dennis Hanks, interview with William H. Herndon, June 13, 1865, *HI*, 37; see also Robert Bray, *Reading with Lincoln* (Carbondale: Southern Illinois University Press, 2010), 1; Nancy M. Theriot, *Mothers and Daughters in Nineteenth Century America: The Biosocial Construction of Femininity* (Lexington: University Press of Kentucky, 1995), 18–20.

17. "Farmers' Wives," *New England Farmer* 5 (1853): 78.

18. Lincoln, "Autobiography Written for John L. Scripps," c. June 1860, *CW* 4:62; Lincoln's reference to his parents' "undistinguished" roots in "To Jesse W. Fell, Enclosing Autobiography," December 20, 1859, ibid., 2: 511.

19. Theriot, *Mothers and Daughters*, 18–23.

20. A. H. Chapman, written statement, September 8, 1865, *HI*, 97.

21. See Louis A. Warren, *Lincoln's Youth: Indiana Years, 1816–1830* (1959; repr., Indianapolis: Indiana Historical Society, 1991), 51, who suggests that Thomas Sparrow was a rather temperamental sort, though there is no direct evidence regarding his character one way or another.

22. See the 1820 Federal Census, Spencer County, Indiana, http://www.census-online.com/links/IN/Spencer/, accessed August 2, 2016; also quite helpful is the genealogical chart of the Grigsby family at http://www.geni.com/people/Reuben-Grigsby/6000000011311288534, accessed October 28, 2015; Nathaniel Grigsby to William H. Herndon, July 4, 1865, *HI*, 70; interview with William H. Herndon, September 12, 1865, ibid., 111–15.

23. On the Brooners' background, see *History of Warrick, Spencer, and Perry Counties*, 557; census information on Wood and his family is from the 1820 Federal Census, Spencer County, Indiana.

24. Esarey, *Indiana Home*, 33–35; Osterud, *Bonds of Community*, chap. 8; John Hanks, interview with John Miles, May 25, 1865, *HI*, 5.

25. John Travis, "Observations on Milk-Sickness," *Western Journal of Medicine and Surgery* 2 (1840): 102.

26. Robert Milham Hartley, *An Historical, Scientific, and Practical Essay on Milk, as an Article of Human Sustenance* (New York: Leavitt Pub., 1842), 269; also Warren, *Lincoln's Youth*, 52.

27. It should be noted here that not everyone agrees Nancy died from milk sickness; some have suggested she in fact died from a particularly virulent strain of tuberculosis, citing an 1870 letter to that effect written by William Herndon. See Emanuel Hertz, *The Hidden Lincoln: From the Letters and Papers of William H. Herndon* (New York: Viking Press, 1938), 74. This is a rather isolated opinion, however; the consensus among Lincoln's friends and family members, many interviewed by Herndon himself, was that milk sickness was the cause of death for Nancy as well as numerous others in the area.

28. Nathaniel Grigsby to William H. Herndon, March 15, 1866, *HI*, 231, mentions the burial of one of the Brooner children with his or her mother, but the child's identity is not given.

29. Dennis Hanks, interview with William H. Herndon, June 13, 1865, *HI*, 40; Nathaniel Grigsby to William H. Herndon, September 4, 1865, ibid., 93; William Wood, interview with William H. Herndon, September 15, 1865, ibid., 123.

30. Dennis Hanks, interview with William H. Herndon, June 13, 1865, *HI*, 40; A. H. Chapman, written statement, September 8, 1865, *HI*, 97; Jonathan Todd Hobson, *Footprints of Abraham Lincoln* (Dayton: Otterbein Press, 1909), 18.

31. Hobson, *Footprints of Abraham Lincoln*, 18.

32. Sophia (or "Sophie") would live with the Lincolns for several years; see Michael Burlingame, *Lincoln : A Life* (Baltimore: Johns Hopkins University Press, 2008), 1:9; Morgan, "New Light on Lincoln's Boyhood," 208–16. In using the Morgan source, I am aware it is even more problematic than usual, for it is based on interviews conducted many years after the events in question; moreover, other sources suggest that Sophie may not have been present in the Lincoln household in 1820 (e.g., the 1820 census contains no mention of her), and in an 1889 interview with Dennis Hanks, he implies that Sophie was not present in the Lincoln household, noting that Sarah Lincoln, Abraham's sister, was the lone "woman" in the house. See Eleanor Atkinson, *The Boyhood of Lincoln* (New York: McClure Co., 1908), 19–20. It is entirely possible, however, that the 1820 census missed Sophie, as she might have been employed as a hired girl on another farm, a common practice, and the 1889 interview may well have been colored by Hanks's old age and other infirmities. In my judgment, the detail and plausibility of the Morgan interview make it a more reliable source.

33. Dennis Hanks, interview with William H. Herndon, June 13, 1865, *HI*, 40.

34. Ibid. Exactly when they began to construct the larger cabin is difficult to ascertain; Hanks's memory seems off here as to dates, for he asserts that the larger cabin was begun in the fall of 1819, but also that this was the same fall when Nancy became ill, which actually occurred in the fall of 1818.

35. William E. Bartlet, *"There I Grew Up": Remembering Abraham Lincoln's Indiana Youth* (Indianapolis: Indiana Historical Society Press, 2008), 22–23, offers a cogent discussion of Thomas's probable time of departure for Kentucky.

36. Sarah Bush Lincoln, interview with William H. Herndon, September 8, 1865, *HI*, 109; Harriet A. Chapman to William H. Herndon, December 17, 1865, ibid., 145.

37. See generally Warren, *Lincoln's Youth*, 60–61; Samuel Haycraft, *A History of Elizabethtown, Kentucky, and Its Surroundings* (Elizabethtown, KY: Woman's Club of Elizabethtown, 1921), 16–17.

38. Morgan, "New Light on Lincoln's Boyhood," 214; "Sarah Bush Johnston Lincoln [Stepmother]," Lincoln Home National Historic Site, Illinois, National Park Service, http://www.nps.gov/liho/learn/historyculture /sarabush.htm, accessed October 30, 2015. John B. Helm to William H. Herndon, August 1, 1865, *HI*, 82, states flatly that Thomas and Dennis Johnston were rivals for Sarah, but Helm's letter is so riddled with exaggerations and errors that his assertions must be treated with skepticism. However, the same assertion is also made by another Elizabethtown resident, Presley Nevil Haycraft to John B. Helm, July 19, 1865, ibid., 87; and by A. H. Chapman, written statement, September 8, 1865, ibid., 98.

39. Samuel Haycraft to William H. Herndon, c. June 1865 and December 7, 1866, *HI*, 68, 503; Samuel Haycraft to John B. Helm, July 5, 1865, ibid., 85.

40. A. H. Chapman, written statement, September 8, 1865, *HI*, 99.

41. Dennis Hanks, interview with William H. Herndon, June 13, 1865, *HI*, 41; Samuel Haycraft to William H. Herndon, c. June 1865, ibid., 68.

42. Morgan, "New Light on Lincoln's Boyhood," 214–15.

43. A. H. Chapman, written statement, September 8, 1865, *HI*, 99.

44. Ibid., 99–100.

45. Ibid., 99; Matilda Johnston Moore, interview with William H. Herndon, September 8, 1865, *HI*, 109.

46. On Sarah's (and the entire Bush family's) lack of education, see John B. Helm to William H. Herndon, August 1, 1865, *HI*, 82; A. H. Chapman, written statement, September 8, 1865, ibid., 99. I speculate that Sarah may have brought these books, because Hanks in his interview

with Herndon mentions no books other than the Bible in the Lincoln cabin until after Sarah's arrival, when he becomes quite specific as to titles; see ibid., 41.

47. Sarah Bush Lincoln, interview with William H. Herndon, September 8, 1865, *HI*, 106–7; John B. Helm to William H. Herndon, August 1, 1865, ibid., 82; A. H. Chapman, written statement, September 8, 1865, ibid., 99.

48. Lincoln, "Autobiography Written for John L. Scripps," c. June 1860, *CW* 4:62.

4. Father and Son

1. Nathaniel Grigsby, interview with William H. Herndon, September 12, 1865, *HI*, 113; Nathaniel Grigsby, Silas Richardson, Nancy Richardson, and John Romine, interview with William H. Herndon, September 14, 1865, ibid., 18; Dennis Hanks, interview with William H. Herndon, June 13, 1865, ibid., 41.

2. Dennis Hanks, interview with William H. Herndon, June 13, 1865, *HI*, 41.

3. For an excellent explanation of Thomas's land purchase arrangement, see Bartelt, *"There I Grew Up,"* 24–25; see also William E. Bartelt, "The Land Dealings of Spencer County, Indiana, Pioneer Thomas Lincoln," *Indiana Magazine of History* 87 (September 1991): 211–23; on the causes and broad economic effects of the 1819 economic crisis, see Murray Newton Rothbard's older but still useful study, *The Panic of 1819: Reactions and Policies* (Auburn, AL: Ludwig von Mises Inst., 1962).

4. Bartelt, *"There I Grew Up,"* 25; see also Thomas H. Greer, "Economic and Social Effects of the Depression of 1819 in the Old Northwest," *Indiana Magazine of History* 44 (September 1948): 227–43.

5. See, e.g., *Laws of the State of Indiana, Passed and Published at the Fourteenth Session of the Indiana General Assembly* (Indianapolis: Smith and Bolton, 1830), 8; Michael B. Katz, *In the Shadow of the Poorhouse: A Social History of Welfare in America* (New York: Basic Books, 1986), 3–36; June Axinn and Mark J. Stern, *Social Welfare: A History of the American Response to Need* (New York: Pearson, 2005); Kayla Hassett, "The County Home in Indiana: A Forgotten Response to Poverty and Disability," master's thesis, Ball State University, 11–12.

6. On the evolution of masculinity and its relation to men's economic roles at this time, see E. Anthony Rotundo, *American Manhood: Transformations in Masculinity from the Revolution to the Modern Era* (New York: Basic Books, 1990), esp. chaps. 8–9; Michael Kimmel, *Manhood in America: A Cultural History* (New York: Oxford University Press, 1998), 11–31.

7. Morris Birkbeck, *Notes on a Journey in America, from the Coast of Virginia to the Territory of Illinois* (London: Severn and Redington, 1816), 80.

8. Dennis F. Hanks, interview with William H. Herndon, June 13, 1865, *HI*, 41.

9. A. H. Chapman, written statement, September 8, 1865, *HI*, 98; Morgan, "New Light on Lincoln's Boyhood," 214–17.

10. Dennis F. Hanks, interview with Erastus Wright, June 8, 1865, *HI*, 28; and interview with William H. Herndon, June 13, 1865, ibid., 40; Samuel Haycraft to William H. Herndon, c. June 1865, ibid., 67; E. R. Burba to William H. Herndon, March 31, 1866, ibid., 240; Nathaniel Grigsby to William H. Herndon, September 4, 1865, ibid., 94. "Country house Carpenter" quote in Samuel Haycraft to John B. Helm, July 5, 1865, ibid., 84; A. H. Chapman, written statement, September 8, 1865, ibid., 98; and William Wood, interview with William H. Herndon, September 15, 1865, ibid., 123.

11. Oliver C. Terry to Jesse W. Weik, July 1888, *HI*, 662–663; Dennis F. Hanks, interview with Erastus Wright, June 8, 1865, ibid., 27.

12. John Hanks, interview with John Miles, May 25, 1865, *HI*, 5; Samuel Haycraft to William H. Herndon, c. June 1865, ibid., 67.

13. "Not nervous" quote from Nathaniel Grigsby, interview with William H. Herndon, September 12, 1865, *HI*, 111; also see his observations about Thomas's contentment, ibid., 113; Dennis F. Hanks, interview with Erastus Wright, June 8, 1865, *HI*, 28; comments about Thomas's generally easygoing character in Hanks, interview with William H. Herndon, June 13, 1865, ibid., 37; A. H. Chapman, written statement, September 8, 1865, ibid., 97.

14. Lincoln, "Autobiography Written for John L. Scripps," c. June 1860, *CW* 4:61.

15. Nathaniel Grigsby, interview with William H. Herndon, September 12, 1865, *HI*, 111.

16. Balch interview in Browne, *Everyday Life of Lincoln*, 86.

17. Lincoln made these remarks to fellow lawyer Leonard Swett; see Don E. Fehrenbacher and Virginia Fehrenbacher, eds., *Recollected Words of Abraham Lincoln* (Palo Alto: Stanford University Press, 1996), 438.

18. A. H. Chapman, written statement, September 8, 1865, *HI*, 97; Browne, *Everyday Life of Lincoln*, 88.

19. Lincoln, "Autobiography Written for John L. Scripps," c. June 1860, *CW* 4:61; Harriet Chapman, interview with Jesse W. Weik, c. 1886–87, *HI*, 646; John Hanks to Jesse W. Weik, June 12, 1887, ibid., 615; see also Sarah Bush Lincoln, interview with William H. Herndon, September 8, 1865, ibid., 107.

20. C. T. Baker, "How Abe Saved the Farm," *Grandview Monitor*, August 26, 1920, reprinted in Bess V. Ehrman, "The Lincoln Inquiry," *Indiana Magazine of History* 21 (March 1925): 10.

21. Ralph LaRossa, *The Modernization of Fatherhood: A Social and Political History* (Chicago: University of Chicago Press, 1997), 25–30, makes these points regarding colonial and Revolutionary-era fatherhood, but they still seem relevant to the largely agrarian environment of southern Indiana in the early nineteenth century.

22. Dennis F. Hanks, interview with Erastus Wright, June 8, 1865, *HI*, 27; A. H. Chapman, written statement, September 8, 1865, ibid., 96.

23. Dennis F. Hanks, interview with Erastus Wright, June 8, 1865, *HI*, 28.

24. Thomas L/D. Johnston, interview with William H. Herndon, c. 1866, *HI*, 532; William G. Greene to William H. Herndon, December 20, 1865, ibid., 145; John Hanks, interview with William H. Herndon, c. 1865–66, ibid., 454; Dennis Hanks, interview with William H. Herndon, June 13, 1865, ibid., 37.

25. On Thomas as an "Old Predestinarian," see A. H. Chapman, written statement, September 8, 1865, *HI*, 97; see also Allen C. Guelzo's discussion of Thomas's faith in *Abraham Lincoln: Redeemer President* (Grand Rapids: William B. Eerdmans Publishing, 1999), 36–38; John Hanks, interview with John Miles, May 25, 1865, *HI*, 5; Dennis F. Hanks, interview with Erastus Wright, June 8, 1865, ibid., 27; John Hanks to Jesse W. Weik, June 12, 1887, ibid., 615; Harriet A. Chapman, interview with Jesse W. Weik, c. 1886–87, ibid., 646.

26. William G. Greene to William H. Herndon, December 20, 1865, *HI*, 145; "white trash" quote in George B. Balch, interview with Jesse W. Weik, c. 1886, ibid., 597; "greenhorn" quote in Presley Nevil Haycraft to John B. Helm, July 19, 1865, ibid., 86; Elbridge Streeter Brooks, *The True Story of Abraham Lincoln, the American* (Boston: Lothrop, Lee, and Shepard, 1896), 16.

27. Lincoln, "To Jesse W. Fell, Enclosing Autobiography," December 20, 1859, *CW* 3:511; and "Autobiography Written for John L. Scripps," c. June 1860, ibid., 4:61; Harriet A. Chapman, interview with Jesse W. Weik, c. 1886–87, *HI*, 646.

28. A. H. Chapman to William H. Herndon, September 28, 1865, *HI*, 134.

29. Dennis F. Hanks to William H. Herndon, January 26, 1866, *HI*, 176; and interview with William H. Herndon, June 13, 1865, ibid., 39.

30. Sarah Bush Lincoln, interview with William H. Herndon, September 8, 1865, *HI*, 107; Lamon, *Life of Abraham Lincoln*, 40.

31. Morgan, "New Light on Lincoln's Boyhood," 214–17.

32. Matilda Johnston Moore, interview with William H. Herndon, September 8, 1865, *HI*, 109; Sarah Bush Lincoln, interview with William

H. Herndon, September 8, 1865, ibid., 107; Joseph C. Richardson, statement for William H. Herndon, c. 1865–66, ibid., 474.

33. John W. Lamar to William H. Herndon, May 18, 1867, *HI*, 560; John B. Helm to William H. Herndon, June 20, 1865, ibid., 48; Lincoln, "Autobiography Written for John L. Scripps," c. June 1860, *CW* 4:62.

34. Lincoln, "Autobiography Written for John L. Scripps," c. June 1860, *CW* 4:62; Elizabeth Crawford to William H. Herndon, February 21, 1866, *HI*, 215.

35. Francis Marion Van Natter, *Lincoln's Boyhood: A Chronicle of His Indiana Years* (Washington, DC: Public Affairs Press, 1963), 36; Sarah Bush Lincoln, interview with William H. Herndon, September 8, 1865, *HI*, 107.

36. Herndon and Weik, *Herndon's Lincoln*, 29.

37. Nathaniel Grigsby, Silas Richardson, Nancy Richardson, John Romine, interview with William H. Herndon, September 14, 1865, *HI*, 118. Lincoln's comparison of his arrangement with his father to that of slavery came in 1856; see Eric Foner, *The Fiery Trial: Abraham Lincoln and American Slavery* (New York: W. W. Norton, 2010), 36.

38. Dennis F. Hanks to William H. Herndon, January 26, 1866, *HI*, 176.

39. Herndon and Weik, *Herndon's Lincoln*, 28n.

40. Lincoln to John D. Johnston and Thomas Lincoln, December 24, 1848, *CW* 2:15–16 (italics in original).

41. Lincoln to John D. Johnson, January 12, 1851, *CW* 2:97.

5. Growing

1. Elizabeth Crawford, interview with William H. Herndon, September 16, 1865, *HI*, 126; Nathaniel Grigsby, interview with William H. Herndon, September 12, 1865, ibid., 113. Grigsby to William H. Herndon, September 4, 1865, ibid., 94, states that Sarah lived with the Grigsby family for two years, but the exact length of time is unknown.

2. On Aaron's background, see "Aaron Grigsby," Kentucky's Abraham Lincoln, Kentucky Historical Society, http://www.lrc.ky.gov/record/Moments09RS/web/Lincoln%20moments%205.pdf, accessed November 2, 2015.

3. A. H. Chapman, written statement, September 8, 1865, *HI*, 100; *Chicago Times Herald*, December 22, 1895, quoted in Doris Kearns Goodwin, *Team of Rivals* (New York: Simon and Schuster, 2005), 49; Lincoln, "Autobiography Written for John L. Scripps," c. June 1860, *CW* 4:61. Aaron outlived his wife by only three years and was buried near her; see Nathaniel Grigsby, Silas Richardson, Nancy Richardson, and John Romine, interview with William H. Herndon, September 14, 1865, *HI*, 118.

4. Dennis Hanks, interview with William H. Herndon, June 13, 1865, *HI*, 43.

5. Morgan, "New Light on Lincoln's Boyhood," 200; Dennis F. Hanks to Abraham Lincoln, April 5, 1864, Abraham Lincoln Papers, Library of Congress, http://memory.loc.gov/cgi-bin/query/r?ammem/mal :@field(DOCID+@lit(d3213400)), accessed November 12, 2015.

6. Morgan, "New Light on Lincoln's Boyhood," 202.

7. Lincoln, "Communication to the People of Sangamo County," March 9, 1832, *CW* 1:8.

8. Text of Northwest Ordinance from the Avalon Project, Lillian Gold-man Law Library, Yale Law School, http://avalon.law.yale.edu/18th _century/nworder.asp, accessed November 5, 2015; Indiana Constitution (1816), Article IX, Sec. 2, text from Indiana Historical Bureau, http://www.in.gov/history/2874.htm, accessed November 5, 2015; see also Richard Gause Boone, *A History of Education in Indiana* (New York: D. Appleton and Co., 1892), 12–14.

9. Boone, *History of Education in Indiana*, 22–24.

10. Joshua Thompson Stewart, *Indiana County, Pennsylvania: Her People Past and Present* (Chicago: J. H. Beers and Co., 1913), 1:197; Timothy Horton Ball, *Northwestern Indiana from 1800 to 1900* (Crown Point, IN: T. H. Ball, 1900), 362–63.

11. Stewart, *Indiana County, Pennsylvania*, 24; Thomas B. Helm, ed., *History of Cass County, Indiana: From the Earliest Times to the Present* (Chicago: Brant and Fuller, 1883), 382–87; Weston Arthur Goodspeed, *Counties of White and Pulaski, Indiana* (Chicago: F. A. Battey and Co., 1883), 619.

12. Boone, *History of Education in Indiana*, 25; "beating" quote in Edward Eggleston, ed., *The Schoolmaster in Literature* (New York: American Book Company, 1892), 561; Lincoln, "To Jesse W. Fell, Enclosing Autobiography," December 20, 1859, *CW* 3:511.

13. Goodspeed, *Counties of White and Pulaski*, 619.

14. Boone, *History of Education in Indiana*, 21.

15. Lincoln, "Autobiography Written for John L. Scripps," c. June 1860, *CW* 4:61; on Riney and Hazel's background, see Burlingame, *Lincoln*, 1:18–19.

16. John Oskins, interview with William H. Herndon, September 16, 1865, *HI*, 128; Lincoln, "Autobiography Written for John L. Scripps," c. June 1860, *CW* 4:62.

17. Burlingame, *Lincoln*, 1:36.

18. Dennis Hanks, interview with William H. Herndon, September 8, 1865, *HI*, 104; Sarah Bush Lincoln, interview with William H. Herndon, September 8, 1865, ibid., 107; John Hanks, interview with William H. Herndon, c. 1865–66, ibid., 455; David Turnham, interview with William H. Herndon, September 15, 1865, ibid., 121; Thomas L. D.

Johnston, interview with William H. Herndon, c. 1866, ibid., 532; the story regarding the grammar book from Morgan, "New Light on Lincoln's Boyhood," 30.

19. Lincoln, "Brief Autobiography," June 15, 1858, *CW* 2:459; "Autobiography Written for John L. Scripps," c. June 1860, ibid., 4:62; Lincoln, "To Jesse W. Fell, Enclosing Autobiography," December 20, 1859, ibid., 3:511. Thomas A. Horrocks, *Lincoln's Campaign Biographies* (Carbondale: Southern Illinois University Press, 2014), 42, 61–62, makes interesting points about the political context of Lincoln's campaign biographies and their descriptions of his education.

20. Bray, *Reading with Lincoln*, 36–40.

21. Dennis F. Hanks, interview with William H. Herndon, June 13, 1865, *HI*, 41; and interview, September 8, 1865, ibid., 105; Elizabeth Crawford, interview with William H. Herndon, September 16, 1865, ibid., 126; Sarah Bush Lincoln, interview with William H. Herndon, September 8, 1865, *HI*, 107; see also Bray, *Reading with Lincoln*, 33–35.

22. Lincoln, "Copybook Verses," c. 1824–26, *CW* 1:1.

23. Sarah Bush Lincoln, interview with William H. Herndon, September 8, 1865, *HI*, 107. Lincoln made the "piece of steel" remark to his close friend Joshua Speed; see Speed to William H. Herndon, December 6, 1866, ibid., 499.

24. Dennis Hanks, interview with William H. Herndon, September 8, 1865, *HI*, 104; Nathaniel Grigsby, Silas Richardson, Nancy Richardson, and John Romine, interview with William H. Herndon, September 14, 1865, ibid., 118 (it is not clear which of these interviewees made this statement); George B. Balch, interview with Jesse W. Weik, c. 1886, ibid., 597.

25. John Hanks, interview with William H. Herndon, c. 1865–66, *HI*, 455; Dennis F. Hanks, interview with William H. Herndon, June 13, 1865, ibid., 41; J. W. Wartmann to William H. Herndon, July 21, 1865, ibid., 79; A. H. Chapman, written statement for William H. Herndon, September 8, 1865, ibid., 101; Oliver C. Terry to Jesse W. Weik, July 1888, ibid., 662; Elizabeth Crawford, interview with William H. Herndon, September 16, 1865, ibid., 125. Elizabeth claimed that her husband made Abraham work only "a day or two" pulling fodder and construed the entire affair in a rather kindlier light than others. John Hanks, interview with William H. Herndon, c. 1865–66, ibid., 455, maintained that the work lasted two or three days.

26. Samuel E. Kercheval to Jesse W. Weik, December 2, 1887, *HI*, 645. Possibly there was some sort of doctrinal dispute between the Grigsbys and the Lincolns in the local Baptist church as well, for later, when the Lincolns were leaving Indiana, the Grigsbys opposed their being given a "letter of dismission"; see Warren, *Lincoln's Youth*, 204–5.

27. Herndon and Weik, *Herndon's Lincoln*, 47–48.

28. Perhaps Josiah Crawford was not terribly amused with Lincoln's satire regarding his nose either, as one neighbor claimed that Crawford went out of his way to get the Lincolns uninvited from the Grigsby wedding; see Joseph C. Richardson, interview with William H. Herndon, September 14, 1865, *HI*, 119.

29. Nathaniel Grigsby, Silas Richardson, Nancy Richardson, and John Romine, interview with William H. Herndon, September 14, 1865, *HI*, 118; S. A. Crawford to William H. Herndon, January 8, 1866, ibid., 154; Green B. Taylor, interview with William H. Herndon, September 16, 1865, ibid., 129; see also Joseph C. Richardson, interview with William H. Herndon, September 14, 1865, ibid., 120.

30. For these alternate stories of the Grigsby fight, see Nathaniel Grigsby to William H. Herndon, October 25, 1865, *HI*, 140; Samuel E. Kercheval to Jesse W. Weik, December 2, 1887, ibid., 645.

31. A. H. Chapman, written statement for William H. Herndon, September 8, 1865, *HI*, 101.

32. For an excellent discussion of this aspect of Lincoln's character, see Michael Burlingame, "Lincoln's Anger and Cruelty," in *The Inner World of Abraham Lincoln* (Urbana: University of Illinois Press, 1994), 147–209.

33. J. Rowan Herndon to William H. Herndon, August 16, 1865, *HI*, 92; William Miller[?], statement for William H. Herndon, September 1866, ibid., 363. For a very cogent and detailed examination of the role wrestling played in American frontier life and Lincoln's early social and political career, see Douglas L. Wilson, *Honor's Voice: The Transformation of Abraham Lincoln* (New York: Vintage Books, 1999), 19–52.

34. Lincoln, "Autobiography Written for John L. Scripps," c. June 1860, *CW* 4:62; Nathaniel Grigsby, Silas Richardson, Nancy Richardson, and John Romine, interview with William H. Herndon, September 14, 1865, *HI*, 118.

35. Joseph C. Richardson, interview with William H. Herndon, September 14, 1865, *HI*, 119; Nathaniel Grigsby, interview with William H. Herndon, September 12, ibid., 112; J. Rowan Herndon to William H. Herndon, August 16, 1865, ibid., 92; David Turnham, interview with William H. Herndon, September 15, 1865, ibid., 120–21; Anna Caroline Gentry, interview with William H. Herndon, September 17, 1865, ibid., 131.

36. Sarah Bush Lincoln, interview with William H. Herndon, September 8, 1865, *HI*, 108; Nathaniel Grigsby, interview with William H. Herndon, September 12, ibid., 113; Nathaniel Grigsby, Silas Richardson, Nancy Richardson, and John Romine, interview with William H. Herndon, September 14, 1865, ibid., 118.

37. Dennis Hanks, interview with William H. Herndon, September 8, 1865, *HI*, 105; Anna Caroline Gentry, interview with William H. Herndon, September 17, 1865, ibid., 131; David Turnham to William H. Herndon, December 17, 1866, ibid., 518.

38. Nathaniel Grigsby, interview with William H. Herndon, September 12, 1865, *HI*, 112; J. Rowan Herndon to William H. Herndon, August 16, 1865, ibid., 92; on his attitude toward animals, see e.g. N. W. Branson to William H. Herndon, August 3, 1865, ibid., 91; Nathaniel Grigsby to William H. Herndon, September 4, 1865, ibid., 94; Matilda Johnson Moore, interview with William H. Herndon, September 8, 1865, ibid., 109.

39. Sarah Bush Lincoln, interview with William H. Herndon, September 8, 1865, *HI*, 108; Absolom Roby, interview with William H. Herndon, September 17, 1865, ibid., 132; Samuel C. Parks to William H. Herndon, March 26, 1866, ibid., 238; Nathaniel Grigsby, interview with William H. Herndon, September 12, 1865, ibid., 114.

40. Nathaniel Grigsby, interview with William H. Herndon, September 12, 1865, *HI*, 112.

41. William Wood, interview with William H. Herndon, September 15, 1865, *HI*, 123. Lincoln was not a particularly zealous temperance advocate and later in life castigated those he thought were excessively so; see his "Temperance Address," February 22, 1842, *CW* 1:271–79.

42. Elizabeth Crawford to William H. Herndon, February 21, 1866, *HI*, 215.

6. Leaving

1. William Wood, interview with William H. Herndon, September 15, 1865, *HI*, 124.

2. Dennis Hanks, interview with William H. Herndon, June 13, 1865, *HI*, 42.

3. A. H. Chapman, statement for William H. Herndon, September 8, 1865, *HI*, 101.

4. William Wood, interview with William H. Herndon, September 15, 1865, *HI*, 123; note the similarities between this and Lincoln, "Address to the Young Men's Lyceum of Springfield, Illinois," January 27, 1838, *CW* 1:108–15.

5. Smith, *Early Indiana Trials and Sketches*, 7.

6. Henry C. Whitney, *Lincoln the Citizen* (New York: Current Literature Pub. Co., 1907), 48; also Warren, *Lincoln's Youth*, 197–98.

7. On Lincoln's supposed early predisposition toward the law as a career, see, e.g., Albert A. Woldman, *Lawyer Lincoln* (New York: Carroll and Graf, 1936), 10–13; John J. Duff, *A. Lincoln, Prairie Lawyer* (New York: Holt, Rinehart and Winston, 1948), 4–8.

8. Dennis Hanks, interview with William H. Herndon, June 13, 1865, *HI*, 42; Joseph C. Richardson, interview with William H. Herndon, September 14, 1865, ibid., 119; Green B. Taylor, interview with William H. Herndon, September 16, 1865, ibid., 129. A. H. Chapman, written statement, September 8, 1865, ibid., 101, states with a somewhat odd certainty that Lincoln never worked the ferry, but multiple other accounts contradict this.

9. See Burlingame, *Lincoln*, 1:34.

10. Several of Lincoln's friends and neighbors later recalled the trip and its circumstances; see, e.g., William G. Greene to William H. Herndon, June 7, 1865, *HI*, 26; Nathaniel Grigsby to William H. Herndon, September 4, 1865, ibid., 94; and interview with Nathaniel Grigsby, September 12, 1865, ibid., 113; on Thomas's trips to New Orleans, see Augustus Chapman, written statement, September 8, 1865, ibid., 100; see also Lincoln to Andrew Johnston, September 6, 1846, *CW* 1:384; for the general context, see Dawn E. Bakken, "A Young Hoosier's Adventures on the Mississippi River," *Indiana Magazine of History* 102 (March 2006): 1–16.

11. Lincoln, "Autobiography Written for John L. Scripps," c. June 1860, *CW* 4:62; see also the recent detailed study by Richard Campanella, *Lincoln in New Orleans: The 1828–1831 Flatboat Voyages and Their Place in History* (Lafayette: University of Louisiana at Lafayette Press, 2010). My own description of this affair is in Dirck, *Lincoln and White America*, 5–24.

12. John Hanks, interview with William H. Herndon, June 13, 1865, *HI*, 43; and interview c. 1865–66, ibid., 456.

13. Dennis F. Hanks, interview with Erastus Wright, June 8, 1865, *HI*, 27.

14. William Wood, interview with William H. Herndon, September 15, 1865, *HI*, 124.

15. David Turnham, interview with William H. Herndon, September 15, 1865, *HI*, 121; also Warren, *Lincoln's Youth*, 204–5.

16. Augustus Chapman, written statement, September 8, 1865, *HI*, 100, 103; Jesse K. DuBois, interview with William H. Herndon, December 1, 1888, ibid., 718.

17. Augustus Chapman, written statement, September 8, 1865, *HI*, 100.

18. Harvey Lee Ross, *The Early Pioneers and Pioneer Events of the State of Illinois* (Chicago: Eastman Bros., 1899), 51.

19. Burlingame, *Lincoln*, 1:50–51; Warren, *Lincoln's Youth*, 208–10.

Epilogue

1. Burlingame, *Lincoln*, 1:50.

2. Hilbert Bennett, "Lincoln in Indiana," *Lincoln Lore*, nos. 271–72 (June 18 and 25, 1934); Lincoln, "Speech at Rockport, Indiana," October 30, 1844, *CW* 1:341.

3. Lincoln to Andrew Johnston, April 18, 1846, *CW* 1:378–79.

4. Lincoln to David Turnham, October 23, 1860, *CW* 4:131.

5. Herndon and Weik, *Herndon's Lincoln*, 244–46; Lincoln, "Speech in Indianapolis, Indiana," September 10, 1859, *CW* 3:463.

6. Lincoln, "Remarks from Balcony of Bates House, Indianapolis," February 11, 1861, *CW* 4:195; see also the excellent and detailed overview of his Indianapolis visit in Harold Holzer, *Lincoln, President-Elect: Abraham Lincoln and the Great Secession Winter, 1860–1861* (New York: Simon and Schuster, 2008), 307–10.

7. Lincoln, "Remarks at Lawrenceburg, Indiana," February 12, 1865, *CW* 4:197.

8. Merrill D. Petersen, *Lincoln in American Memory* (New York: Oxford University, 1994), 19.

9. Ibid., 19–20; see also "The Lincoln Funeral Train," Indiana Historical Bureau, http://www.in.gov/history/markers/Ltrain.htm, accessed February 4, 2016.

10. Dave Stafford, "Indiana Lincoln Funeral Train Commemorations Planned," The Indiana Lawyer, http://www.theindianalawyer.com/article/print?articleId=36907, accessed February 4, 2016.

BIBLIOGRAPHY

Affleck, Thomas, ed. *The Western Farmer and Gardener, Devoted to Agriculture, Horticulture, and Rural Economy.* Vol. 2, *From October, 1840, to September, 1841.* Cincinnati: Charles Foster, 1841.

Angle, Paul M., ed. *The Lincoln Reader.* New York: DaCapo Press, 1946.

Anson, Bert. *The Miami Indians.* Norman: University of Oklahoma Press, 1970.

Atkinson, Eleanor. *The Boyhood of Lincoln.* New York: McClure Co., 1908.

Axinn, June, and Mark J. Stern. *Social Welfare: A History of the American Response to Need.* New York: Pearson, 2005.

Baker, Ronald L. *Hoosier Folk Legends.* Bloomington: Indiana University Press, 1982.

Bakken, Dawn E. "A Young Hoosier's Adventures on the Mississippi River." *Indiana Magazine of History* 102 (March 2006): 1–16.

Ball, Timothy Horton. *Northwestern Indiana from 1800 to 1900.* Crown Point, IN: T. H. Ball, 1900.

Barr, Arvil S. "A History of Warrick County, Indiana, Prior to 1820, Including a Sketch of Methodism in the County down to 1850." Master's thesis, University of Indiana, 1915.

Barrett, Joseph H. *Life of Abraham Lincoln.* Cincinnati: Moore, Wilstach, and Baldwin, 1864.

Bartelt, William E. "The Land Dealings of Spencer County, Indiana, Pioneer Thomas Lincoln," *Indiana Magazine of History* 87 (September 1991): 211–23.

———. *"There I Grew Up": Remembering Abraham Lincoln's Indiana Youth.* Indianapolis: Indiana Historical Society Press, 2008.

Bennett, Hilbert. "Lincoln in Indiana." *Lincoln Lore.* Nos. 271–72 (June 18 and 25, 1934).

Biographical and Historical Record of Kosciusko County, Indiana. Chicago: Lewis Pub. Co., 1887.

Birkbeck, Morris. *Notes on a Journey in America, from the Coast of Virginia to the Territory of Illinois.* London: Severn and Redington, 1816.

Boone, Richard Gause. *A History of Education in Indiana.* New York: D. Appleton and Co., 1892.

Bray, Robert. *Reading with Lincoln.* Carbondale: Southern Illinois University Press, 2010.

Brooks, Elbridge Streeter. *The True Story of Abraham Lincoln, the American.* Boston: Lothrop, Lee, and Shepard, 1896.

Brown, Kent Masterson. "Report on the Title of Thomas Lincoln to, and the History of, the Lincoln Boyhood Home along Knob Creek in LaRue

County, Kentucky." https://archive.org/stream/reportontitleoft00brow /reportontitleoft00brow_djvu.txt, accessed October 21, 2015.

Browne, Frances Fisher. *The Everyday Life of Abraham Lincoln*. 1886. Reprint, Lincoln: University of Nebraska Press, 1995.

Burlingame, Michael. *The Inner World of Abraham Lincoln*. Urbana: University of Illinois Press, 1994.

———. *Lincoln: A Life*. 2 vols. Baltimore: Johns Hopkins University Press, 2008.

Campanella, Richard. *Lincoln in New Orleans: The 1828–1831 Flatboat Voyages and Their Place in History*. Lafayette: University of Louisiana at Lafayette Press, 2010.

Cockrum, William Monroe. *Pioneer History of Indiana: Including Stories, Incidents, and Customs of the Early Settlers*. Oakland City, IN: Press of Oakland City, 1907.

Coulter, Stanley. *Forest Trees of Indiana*. Indianapolis: Wm. B. Burford, 1892.

Cox, Sandford C. *Recollections of the Early Settlement of the Wabash Valley*. Lafayette, IN: Courier, 1860.

Crawford, Mary M., ed. "Mrs. Lydia B. Bacon's Journal, 1811–1812." *Indiana Magazine of History* 40 (December 1944): 367–86.

Cressy, Benjamin Cothen. *An Appeal in Behalf of the Indiana Theological Seminary, Located at South Hanover, Indiana*. Boston: Pierce and Parker, 1832.

Danhof, Clarence H. *Changes in Agriculture: The Northern United States, 1820–1870*. Cambridge, MA: Harvard University Press, 1970.

Dippel, John V. H. *Race to the Frontier: "White Flight" and Westward Expansion*. New York: Algora Pub., 2005.

Dirck, Brian R. *Abraham Lincoln and White America*. Lawrence: University Press of Kansas, 2012.

———. *Lincoln the Lawyer*. Urbana: University of Illinois Press, 2007.

Drez, Ronald J. *The War of 1812, Conflict and Deception*. Baton Rouge: Louisiana State University Press, 2014.

Duff, John J. *A. Lincoln, Prairie Lawyer*. New York: Holt, Rinehart and Winston, 1948.

Eggleston, Edward, ed. *The Schoolmaster in Literature*. New York: American Book Company, 1892.

Ehrman, Bess V. "The Lincoln Inquiry." *Indiana Magazine of History* 21 (March 1925): 10–14.

Ellsworth, Henry William. *Valley of the Upper Wabash, Indiana, with Hints on Its Agricultural Advantages*. New York: Pratt, Robinson, and Co., 1838.

Esarey, Logan. *A History of Indiana, from Its Exploration to 1850*. Vol. 1. Indianapolis: B. F. Bowen, 1918.

———, ed. *Indiana Historical Collections*, vol. 9: *Governor's Messages and Letters*, vol. 2. Indianapolis: Indiana Historical Commission, 1922.

——. *The Indiana Home*. Bloomington: Indiana University Press, 1953.

Fanshaw, Daniel. *Twenty-First Annual Report of the American Tract Society*. New York: American Tract Society, 1846.

"Farmers' Wives," *New England Farmer* 5 (1853): 78.

Faux, William. *Memorable Days in America*. 1823. Reprint, Carlisle, PA: Applewood Books, 2007.

Fehrenbacher, Don E., and Virginia Fehrenbacher, eds. *Recollected Words of Abraham Lincoln*. Palo Alto: Stanford University Press, 1996.

Flint, James. *Letters from America*. London: Longman, Hurst, Reese, Orme, and Brown, 1822.

Foner, Eric. *The Fiery Trial: Abraham Lincoln and American Slavery*. New York: W. W. Norton, 2010.

Fraysse, Oliver. *Lincoln, Land, and Labor, 1809–1860*. Urbana: University of Illinois Press, 1988.

Glenn, Elizabeth, and Stewart Rafert. *The Native Americans*. Indianapolis: Indiana Historical Society Press, 2009.

Goodspeed, Weston Arthur. *Counties of White and Pulaski, Indiana*. Chicago: F. A. Battey and Co., 1883.

Goodwin, Doris Kearns. *Team of Rivals*. New York: Simon and Schuster, 2005.

Gray, Ralph D., ed. *Indiana History: A Book of Readings*. Bloomington: Indiana University Press, 1994.

Greer, Thomas H. "Economic and Social Effects of the Depression of 1819 in the Old Northwest." *Indiana Magazine of History* 44 (September 1948): 227–43.

Groneman, Carol, and Mary Beth Norton, eds. *"To Toil the Livelong Day": America's Women at Work, 1780–1980*. Ithaca, NY: Cornell University Press, 1987.

Guelzo, Allen C. *Abraham Lincoln: Redeemer President*. Grand Rapids: William B. Eerdmans Publishing, 1999.

Gunn, John C. *Gunn's Domestic Medicine; or, Poor Man's Friend*. 13th ed. Pittsburgh: J. Edwards, 1839.

Hareven, Tamara K., and Maris A. Vinovskis, eds. *Family and Population in Nineteenth Century America*. Princeton, NJ: Princeton University Press, 1978.

Harris, Branson L. *Some Recollections of My Boyhood*. Indianapolis: Hollenbeck Press, 1900.

Harrison, Lowell H. *Kentucky's Road to Statehood*. Lexington: University Press of Kentucky, 1992.

——. *Lincoln of Kentucky*. Lexington: University Press of Kentucky, 2000.

Hartley, Robert Milham. *An Historical, Scientific, and Practical Essay on Milk, as an Article of Human Sustenance*. New York: Leavitt Pub., 1842.

Hassett, Kayla. "The County Home in Indiana: A Forgotten Response to Poverty and Disability." Master's thesis, Ball State University, 2013.

Haycraft, Samuel. *A History of Elizabethtown, Kentucky, and Its Surroundings*. Elizabethtown, KY: Woman's Club of Elizabethtown, 1921.

Helm, Thomas B., ed. *History of Cass County, Indiana: From the Earliest Times to the Present*. Chicago: Brant and Fuller, 1883.

Herndon, William H., and Jesse W. Weik, *Herndon's Lincoln*. 1889. Reprint, Urbana: University of Illinois Press, 2006.

Hertz, Emmanuel. *The Hidden Lincoln: From the Letters and Papers of William H. Herndon*. New York: Viking Press, 1938.

History of Fayette County, Indiana. Chicago: Warner, Beers and Co., 1886.

History of Miami County, Indiana. Chicago: Brant and Fuller, 1887.

History of Warrick, Spencer, and Perry Counties, Indiana. Chicago: Goodspeed Bros., 1885.

Hobson, Jonathan Todd. *Footprints of Abraham Lincoln*. Dayton: Otterbein Press, 1909.

Hoch, Bradley R. *The Lincoln Trail in Pennsylvania: A History and Guide*. University Park: Pennsylvania State University Press, 2001.

Holzer, Harold. *Lincoln, President-Elect: Abraham Lincoln and the Great Secession Winter, 1860–1861*. New York: Simon and Schuster, 2008.

Horrocks, Thomas A. *Lincoln's Campaign Biographies*. Carbondale: Southern Illinois University Press, 2014.

Howells, William Dean. *Life of Abraham Lincoln*. Springfield, IL: Abraham Lincoln Assoc., 1938.

Jefferson, Thomas. *Notes on the State of Virginia*. New York: Palgrave, 2002.
———. *The Writings of Thomas Jefferson*. Edited by H. A. Washington. 9 vols. New York: H. W. Derby, 1861.

Jensen, Joan M. *Loosening the Bonds: Mid-Atlantic Farm Women, 1750–1850*. New Haven, CT: Yale University Press, 1986.

Johnson, Samuel Roosevelt. *O Worship the Lord in the Beauty of Holiness: A Sermon at the Consecration of St. Mary's Church, Delphi, Indiana*. New York: Stanford and Swords, 1845.

Jones, Thomas P., ed. *Journal of the Franklin Institute of the State of Pennsylvania*. Philadelphia: J. Harding, 1835.

Katz, Michael B. *In the Shadow of the Poorhouse: A Social History of Welfare in America*. New York: Basic Books, 1986.

Kimmel, Michael. *Manhood in America: A Cultural History*. New York: Oxford University Press, 1998.

Kinley, Isaac. "Education of the Farmer." In *Second Annual Report of the Indiana State Board of Agriculture*, 359–66. Indianapolis: J. P. Chapman, 1853.

Lamon, Ward Hill. *The Life of Abraham Lincoln from His Birth to His Inauguration as President*. Bedford, MA: Applewood Books, 1872.

LaRossa, Ralph. *The Modernization of Fatherhood: A Social and Political History*. Chicago: University of Chicago Press, 1997.

Laws of the State of Indiana, Passed and Published at the Fourteenth Session of the Indiana General Assembly. Indianapolis: Smith and Bolton, 1830.

Lewis, George E. *The Indiana Land Company, 1763–1798: A Study in Eighteenth-Century Frontier Land Speculation and Business Venture*. Glendale, CA: Arthur H. Clark Co., 1941.

Lincoln, Abraham. *The Collected Works of Abraham Lincoln*. Edited by Roy P. Basler. 9 vols. New Brunswick, NJ: Rutgers University Press, 1953–1955.

Madison, James H. *The Indiana Way: A State History*. Bloomington: Indiana University Press, 1986.

McMurtry, R. Gerald. "The Lincoln Migration from Kentucky to Indiana." *Indiana Magazine of History* 33 (December 1937): 385–421.

Moore, Edward E., comp. *Moore's Hoosier Cyclopedia*. Indianapolis: Press of Wm. B. Burford, 1905.

Moores, Charles. "Old Corydon." *Indiana Magazine of History* 13 (March 1917): 20–41.

Morgan, Arthur E. "New Light on Lincoln's Boyhood." *Atlantic Monthly* 125 (February 1920): 208–18.

"Mr. Holmes." "Excerpt from the Maine *Farmer*, 'Culture of Roots, Silk, etc.'" *American Railroad Journal, and Advocate of Internal Improvements* 5 (1836): 520.

Olmstead, Frederick Law. *The Cotton Kingdom: A Traveler's Observations on Cotton and Slavery in the American Slave States*. New York: Mason Bros., 1862.

Osterud, Nancy Grey. *Bonds of Community: The Lives of Farm Women in Nineteenth-Century New York*. Ithaca, NY: Cornell University Press, 1991.

Pessen, Edward. *Jacksonian America: Society, Personality, and Politics*. Urbana: University of Illinois Press, 1985.

Petersen, Merrill D. *Lincoln in American Memory*. New York: Oxford University Press, 1994.

Rose, Gregory S. "The Distribution of Indiana's Ethnic and Racial Minorities in 1850." *Indiana Magazine of History* 87 (September 1991): 224–60.

Ross, Harvey Lee. *The Early Pioneers and Pioneer Events of the State of Illinois*. Chicago: Eastman Bros., 1899.

Rothbard, Murray Newton. *The Panic of 1819: Reactions and Policies*. Auburn, AL: Ludwig von Mises Inst., 1962.

Rotundo, E. Anthony. *American Manhood: Transformations in Masculinity from the Revolution to the Modern Era*. New York: Basic Books, 1990.

Sakolski, Aaron M. *The Great American Land Bubble: The Amazing Story of Land-Grabbing, Speculations, and Booms from Colonial Days to the Present Time*. 1932. Reprint, New York: Martino, 2011.

Salstrom, Paul. *From Pioneering to Persevering: Family Farming in Indiana to 1880*. Lafayette, IN: Purdue University Press, 2007.

Scott, James Leander. *A Journal of a Missionary Tour through Pennsylvania, Ohio, Indiana, Illinois, Iowa, Wiskonsin, and Michigan*. Providence, RI: J. L. Scott, 1843.

Scott, John. *The Indiana Gazetteer*. 2nd ed. Indianapolis: Douglas and Maguire, 1833.

Searle, Thomas C. "Dutch Settlement in Indiana." *The Christian Spectator* 2 (November 1820): 609–11. New Haven, CT: Howe and Spalding, 1820.

Smith, Oliver Hampton. *Early Indiana Trials and Sketches: Reminiscences by Hon. O. H. Smith*. Cincinnati: Moore, Wilstach, Keys and Co., 1858.

Stafford, Dave. "Indiana Lincoln Funeral Train Commemorations Planned." The Indiana Lawyer. http://www.theindianalawyer.com/article/print?articleId=36907, accessed February 4, 2016.

Steinson, Barbara J. "Rural Life in Indiana, 1800–1950." *Indiana Magazine of History* 90 (September 1994): 203–50.

Stevens, Frank E. "Illinois in the War of 1812–1814." In *Transactions of the Illinois State Historical Society for the Year 1904*, 62–197. Springfield, IL: Phillips Bros., 1904.

Stewart, Joshua Thompson. *Indiana County, Pennsylvania: Her People Past and Present*. 2 vols. Chicago: J. H. Beers and Co., 1913.

Swierenga, Robert P. "Land Speculation and Its Impact on American Economic Growth and Welfare: A Historiographical Review." *Western Historical Quarterly* 8 (July 1977): 283–302.

Tarbell, Ida. *Abraham Lincoln and His Ancestors*. New York: Harper and Bros., 1924.

Taylor, Robert M., and Connie A. McBirney. *Peopling Indiana: The Ethnic Experience*. Indianapolis: Indiana Historical Society, 1996.

Theriot, Nancy M. *Mothers and Daughters in Nineteenth Century America: The Biosocial Construction of Femininity*. Lexington: University Press of Kentucky, 1995.

Todd, Sereno Edwards. *The Young Farmer's Manual*. New York: F. W. Woodward, 1867.

Travis, John. "Observations on Milk-Sickness." *Western Journal of Medicine and Surgery* 2 (1840): 102–8.

Van Natter, Francis Marion. *Lincoln's Boyhood: A Chronicle of His Indiana Years*. Washington, DC: Public Affairs Press, 1963.

Waltmann, Henry G. *Pioneer Farming in Indiana: Thomas Lincoln's Major Crops*. Washington, DC: Smithsonian Institution, 1975.

Warren, Louis A. *Lincoln's Youth: Indiana Years, 1816–1830*. 1959. Reprint, Indianapolis: Indiana Historical Society, 1991.

Weik, Jesse W. *Weik's History of Putnam County, Indiana*. Indianapolis: B. F. Bowen, 1910.

Whitney, Henry C. *Lincoln the Citizen*. New York: Current Literature Pub. Co., 1907.

Wied, Maximilian. *Travels in the Interior of North America*. London: Ackerman and Co., 1843.

Wilson, Douglas L. *Honor's Voice: The Transformation of Abraham Lincoln*. New York: Vintage Books, 1999.

Wilson, Douglas L., and Rodney O. Davis, eds. *Herndon's Informants: Letters, Interviews, and Statements about Abraham Lincoln*. Urbana: University of Illinois Press, 1998.

Wilson, William E. *The Angel and the Serpent: The Story of New Harmony*. Bloomington: Indiana University Press, 1964.

———. *Indiana: A History*. Bloomington: Indiana University Press, 1966.

Winger, Otho. *History of the Church of the Brethren in Indiana*. Elgin, IL: Brethren Publishing House, 1917.

Woldman, Albert A. *Lawyer Lincoln*. New York: Carroll and Graf, 1936.

Woods, John. *Two Years' Residence in the Settlement on the English Prairie, in the Illinois Country, United States*. London: A. and R. Spottiswoode, 1822.

Woollen, William Wesley. *Biographical and Historical Sketches of Early Indiana*. Indianapolis: Hammond and Co., 1883.

Young, Andrew White. *History of Wayne County, Indiana, from Its First Settlement to the Present Time*. Cincinnati: Robert Clarke and Co., 1872.

INDEX

Brian R. Dirck is a professor of history at Anderson University in Indiana. He is the author of numerous books and articles on Abraham Lincoln and the Civil War era, including *Lincoln and Davis: Imagining America, 1809–1865*; *Lincoln the Lawyer*; *Lincoln and the Constitution*; and *Abraham Lincoln and White America*.

CONCISE
LINCOLN
LIBRARY

This series of concise books fills a need for short studies of the life, times, and legacy of President Abraham Lincoln. Each book gives readers the opportunity to quickly achieve basic knowledge of a Lincoln-related topic. These books bring fresh perspectives to well-known topics, investigate previously overlooked subjects, and explore in greater depth topics that have not yet received book-length treatment. For a complete list of current and forthcoming titles, see www.conciselincolnlibrary.com.

Other Books in the Concise Lincoln Library